PROPHECY

✳

SYLVIA BROWNE

with
Lindsay Harrison

PROPHECY

What the Future Holds for You

DOUBLEDAY LARGE PRINT HOME LIBRARY EDITION

DUTTON

This Large Print Edition, prepared especially for Doubleday Large Print Home Library, contains the complete, unabridged text of the original Publisher's Edition.

DUTTON

Published by Penguin Group (USA) Inc.
375 Hudson Street, New York, New York 10014, U.S.A.
Penguin Books Ltd, Registered Offices: 80 Strand,
London WC2R 0RL, England
Penguin Books Australia Ltd, 250 Camberwell Road,
Camberwell, Victoria 3124, Australia
Penguin Books Canada Ltd, 10 Alcorn Avenue, Toronto,
Ontario, Canada M4V 3B2
Penguin Books (NZ) Ltd, Cnr Rosedale and Airborne Roads,
Albany, Auckland 1310, New Zealand

Published by Dutton, a member of Penguin Group (USA) Inc.

 REGISTERED TRADEMARK—MARCA REGISTRADA

ISBN: 0-7394-4486-7

Printed in the United States of America

This Large Print Book carries the
Seal of Approval of N.A.V.H.

From Sylvia and Lindsay—
This one's for Bonnie Solow.
A very long thank-you note.

CONTENTS

✳

PART III. OUR PHYSICAL, EMOTIONAL,
MENTAL AND SPIRITUAL HEALTH

INTRODUCTION

*

I was eighteen years old. I'd been psychic for eighteen years, but I still hadn't made peace with it. I was starting to do readings for people, successfully, and I was even building a clientele, to my amazement. The problem was, while I never doubted my God-given ability to see into people's futures (I didn't especially appreciate it, but I never doubted it), I kept hoping that somehow none of these new clients would notice that, accurate or not, I didn't especially know what I was doing or how I was doing it. Except for my much adored and brilliantly psychic Grandma Ada, I had no one to talk to about it, no one to ask advice from or express my insecurities to or, probably most of all, tremble to about the responsibility of people turning to me for insights and warnings about what their lives held in store.

And so, I began reading everything I could get my hands on about other people who'd seemed to be "like me," communicating with spirits, seeing clients, peering into the future, using their gifts for other people's benefit and trying to serve God in the process. Somewhere between a biography of Madame Helena Blavatsky and one of Edgar Cayce's many books I became intrigued with the idea of expanding my visions of the future from one client at a time to the world at large, just like Cayce and Madame Blavatsky and Sir Arthur Conan Doyle and so many others I was reading about had done, with often remarkable accuracy.

I wasn't very ceremonious about it. I just sat down one day, surrounded myself with the White Light of the Holy Spirit to keep God's presence and protection around me, told Him what I was about to do (as if He didn't know) and prayed for His wisdom and insights as I looked into the future of life on earth, took a deep meditative breath and nearly fainted. The rush of images and sounds and flashes and special effects and explosions and music and words and cars and doctors and rocket ships—it was like seeing and hearing every movie you've ever sat through, all at the same time, superimposed over one another.

Needless to say, I put a stop to that very quickly, and realized that if I was ever going to be able to expand my gift to anything beyond one-on-one prophecies, I was going to have to find a way to organize those prophecies into some kind of sequence my mind could sort out and make sense of. After a bit of trial and error early on, I finally learned that breaking prophecies down into one subject at a time—focusing on that one subject and then stepping aside for whatever information comes in—was what worked best for me.

Which explains the structure you'll find in the pages of this book. As some of you may know, I have "standing dates" on several television and radio shows to do annual New Year's predictions for the coming year. Those are great fun, and I enjoy them and am thrilled to be accurate enough that they keep inviting me back. But this book, subject by subject rather than year by year, is written at my real "comfort level" and my ultimate pleasure when it comes to prophecies.

I hesitate to call them "my" prophecies, because again, ultimately, everything comes from God. That doesn't mean you should read these prophecies as a series of divine messages directly from Him. As you'll read in Chapter 3, prophecies have a variety of sources, all of which trace back to our Creator, but by the time we fallible humans have finished translating them and communicating them, we're bound to get it wrong some of the time.

I simply meant to acknowledge that never do I write a book, do a reading, give a lecture, make a media appearance, appear at a book signing or, for that matter, even take a breath, without God and His love at its core.

I thank Him for being with me through every page of writing *Prophecy,* and with you through every page of reading it.

—Sylvia C. Browne

PROPHECY

✳

CHAPTER ONE

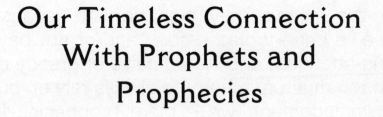

Our Timeless Connection With Prophets and Prophecies

It is our nature to want to know what the future holds. From the moment we first began to inhabit this earth in human form, we've believed that forewarned is forearmed, and we've sought out those who seem to have a clearer view of the road ahead than we do. On a small scale, we don't want to get caught in the rain without an umbrella, but we also wouldn't mind knowing whether or not we should save that rainwater for an upcoming drought or man-made crisis. On a much larger scale, we want to know that we personally, we as a community, we as a faith, as a society, as a nation or as a surprisingly fragile planet are going to be okay and, more to the point, what "okay" is going to look like. We look to prophets and prophecies not just for warnings but also for hope and for comfort, no matter how far in the distance they might be. And because we've been fooled before, and/or not paying attention, and/or too naive or greedy or in too much of a hurry to always rely on our own judgment, we explore prophecies in search of a blueprint for discerning the real from the counterfeit, the truth from the lies, the heroes from the villains, meaningful road signs from time- and soul-wasting detours and, probably most essential of all, the genuinely God-centered from the countless clever pretenders.

The Cultural Bond of Prophecy

One of the countless aspects of prophets and prophecies that has always fascinated me is that they've always been traditional and fundamental to civilizations throughout the world, even the most ancient, isolated cultures who had no interest in or means of communicating with each other. It's not as if the Aborigines of Australia heard that predicting the long-range future had become very popular among American Indians and decided to give it a try, or the Mayans only started coming up with prophecies so they wouldn't be outdone by those Egyptian prophets they kept hearing about. Cultures tend to express the most deep-rooted essences of their people, and each of these cultures, so vastly different in so many ways, has demonstrated, separately and together, that we're eternally united as human beings around the world in our insistence that the future is *knowable.*

Of course, the future *is* knowable, and I'll explain in Chapter 3 exactly why that is. That fact alone, and our universal agreement that it's true, should bring us more peace than it does. Who's "good at" and "bad at" foreseeing the future, and which information is accurate and which isn't, is almost beside the point when it comes to simply appreciating how dearly held our global yearning to look ahead really is. It would be impossible to explore the prophecies of every culture that ever existed, or that exists today, but I want to highlight just a few, hoping that as you read them you'll focus on the respectful purity of spirit at their core, no matter what corner of the world they came from.

The American Indians

A friend of mine was involved in a recent documentary about native American Indians. The film crew shot for a couple of weeks, capturing great footage of several generations of the tribes they were focused on, their rituals, their daily lives, their traditions and ceremonies, their relationships within families and within the tribe, and the extent to which "civilization" had irreversibly seeped into their lives.

As wonderful as the footage and the camera work were, though, and as mesmerizing as that collage of brown, beautiful faces from ages one year old to a hundred were to watch, the producers and the director realized that their film was still missing something, some special element that would set it apart from every other documentary ever done about the American Indian. As a solution, someone came up with the idea of giving a camera to the Indians themselves and letting them shoot some footage, so the makers of the documentary could really get a look at life through the eyes of the subjects of their film. And that's exactly what they did.

A week later the producers and director found themselves gaping, with chagrin at first, at the results of their bright idea: a coyote's pawprints in a muddy riverbank, a wisp of white fur caught in a broken branch, a hawk circling, an aura around a full moon, an approaching thunderstorm, a bear catching fish in a waterfall, a wolf loping across a hill—hour after hour of footage, and not for one second was there so much as a glimpse of a human being.

What they finally edited together was a gorgeous documentary and eloquent, simple proof of what's been written about American Indians for thousands of years: ask them to tell you their story and they'll tell you about Nature.

Of course, the many tribes of the native American nations each have their own distinct language, customs and cherished legacy of prophecies. But even their prophecies reflect their reverence for this earth and our essential spiritual connection to it, without which humankind can't and won't survive. One of the most beautiful examples is an excerpt from a Lakota prophecy. It refers to the Star People, whom many tribes believe to be their ancient extraterrestrial ancestors, and to the Sacred Mother, who is the earth:

In the next decade, the Star People that you call meteorites will come to this earth in answer to the Mother's call for help. You see, we are all relations. So the Star People are beings, and they are the planets, and the other bodies in the heavens as well.

The Sacred Mother is screaming for life and the meteorites will hear her cries and answer her call for help. They will hit the earth from the heavens with such force that many internal things will happen as well as external. The earth will move as a result of the impact. This will cause the sacred fire that is the source of all life to the Mother to move through her body.

The rains will change their fall and the winds will alter their course and what has existed for three hundred years will no longer exist. And where there is summer, there will be fall. And where there is fall, there will be winter. And where there is winter, there will be spring.

The animals and plants will become confused. There will be great plagues that you do not understand. Many of these plagues are born from your scientists whose intentions have gone awry. Your scientists have let these monsters loose upon the land. These plagues will spread through your waters and through your blood and through your food because you have disrupted the natural chain through which your Mother cleanses herself.

Only those who have learned to live on the land will find sanctuary. Go to where the eagles fly, to where the wolf roams, to where the bear lives. Here you will find life because they will always go to where the water is pure and the air can be breathed. Live where the trees, the lungs of this earth, purify the air. There is a time coming, beyond the weather. The veil between the physical and the spiritual world is thinning.

And this came from Brave Buffalo of the Brule Sioux Nation:

It is time for the Great Purification. We are at a point of no return. The two-legged are about to bring destruction to life on earth. It's happened before, and it's about to happen again. The Sacred Hoop shows how all things go in a circle. The old becomes new; the new becomes old. Everything repeats. White people have no culture. Culture is having roots in the earth. People without culture don't exist very long because Nature is God. Without a connection to Nature, the people drift, grow negative, destroy themselves. In the beginning we had one mind, and it was positive, a thing of beauty, seeing beauty everywhere.

The Aborigines

Half a world away from the American Indians, and very probably unaware of their existence, the Australian Aborigines are thought to have been on this earth for more than eighteen thousand generations. From

their ancient beginnings they've been no-
madic hunters and gatherers, traveling and
living in clans, orally passing their culture
and traditions along from one generation to
the next to the next to the next. They revere
Nature and their elders, they're intensely
connected to both the practical and the
spiritual sides of their lives, and they embrace a gorgeous mythology called the
"Dreamtime" that lies at the heart of their
belief system.

The Dreamtime, which is woven through
Aboriginal lives in a variety of daily applications, is at its core their treasured account of
that time when their spirit ancestors moved
through the bare, unsanctified land and
gave it its physical form and its sacred laws.
There was the Rainbow Serpent who slith-
ered across the world creating rivers and
valleys with its massive body. Bila was the
sun woman whose fire lit the world. She was
destroyed by two lizardlike creatures called
Kudna and Muda, who, frightened by the
darkness they'd brought about by killing
Bila, began hurling boomerangs into the sky
in all directions, trying to bring back the light.
Kudna's boomerang flew into the eastern
sky and a brilliant ball of fire appeared,

which slowly crossed the sky and vanished again beyond the western horizon, and day and night were born. The countless spirits and stories are the exquisite foundation on which the Aborigines build their reverent awe of all of Nature and their belief that it is humankind's privilege to live among and serve such hallowed creations.

Dreamtime is a tangible reality of the Aboriginal past, present and future. It isn't something that happened a very long time ago and was completed, it's an ongoing consciousness and responsibility with tragic consequences if it's ignored. A prophecy from an Australian Aboriginal Tribal Elder named Guboo Ted Thomas, orally preserved until it was committed to writing, reflects their profoundly simple faith:

I was in Dreamtime.
I see this great wave going.
I tell people about this wave.
It wasn't a tidal wave.
This was a spiritual wave.
So, to me, I believe that the Dreamtime
    is going to be that.
I believe the revival is going to start in
    Australia when we're Dreaming.

It's the hummingbee that I'm talking
about.
And love.
We've got to learn to love one another.
You see, that's really what's going to
happen to the earth.
We're going to have tidal waves.
We're going to have earthquakes.
That's coming because we don't
consider this land as our Mother.
We've taken away the balance, and
we're not putting back.
I look at the bush, and those trees are
alive.
They're not dead, they're alive.
And they want you to cuddle them.

The Incas

Thousands of miles from the American Indians and the Australian Aborigines, the ancient Inca civilization evolved on the South American continent. The origins of the Incas are a mystery, primarily recorded through the oral legacy of a people whose world was destroyed and whose vast wealth was pirated by Spanish conquistadors in 1532.

At its most powerful, the Inca Empire was the largest nation on earth, stretching 2500 miles along the Andes Mountains. They were artisans, hunters, gatherers, farmers and incredibly gifted builders and engineers, constructing more than fourteen thousand miles of roads before such a thing as the wheel even existed, roads built for foot travel but so time- and weather-resistant that some of them are still virtually intact today. Also still intact today, and marveled over by visitors from around the world, are Inca pyramids, temples, observatories and some structures that were never finished, mute reminders of lives interrupted forever and a brilliant civilization thrown aside for power and greed.

Nature formed the heart of the Inca language and the Inca religion as well. The Incas believed that all creation in nature was the work of the Sun God, and they considered themselves to be descendants of the Sun. They held festivals at the end of every harvest season to thank the Sun God for their bountiful crops or to pray for better crops in the season ahead, and at the solstices when the earth and the Sun are at their farthest from each other, the Incas held ceremonies to ask the Sun God not to leave his children. They believed in reincarnation and even carried the mummies of revered ancestors to the holiest of rituals so their ancestors could share the events with them.

After the Inca civilization was destroyed in the 1500s, a small tribe of refugees called the Q'ero escaped to isolated villages in the high Andes. They've lived there ever since, with the Q'ero elders and shamans passing along the Inca language, history, traditions and prophecies to five hundred years of descendants.

The Western world's first actual sighting of the Q'ero villages didn't happen until 1955. Communication between the Westerners and the Q'ero evolved from there, and in 1996 a tribal leader, the head shaman and other Q'ero elders honored the United States with a historic visit in which, among other shared knowledge and rituals, they passed along the prophecies of their revered Inca ancestors. Those prophecies read, in part:

The new caretakers of the Earth will come from the West, and those that have made the greatest impact on Mother Earth now have the moral responsibility to remake their relationship with her, after remaking themselves.

The prophecy holds that North America will supply the physical strength, or body; Europe will supply the mental aspect, or head; and the heart will be supplied by South America.

The prophecies are optimistic.

They refer to the end of time as we know it—the death of a way of thinking and a way of being, the end of a way of relating to nature and to the earth.

In the coming years, the Incas expect us to emerge into a golden age, a golden millennium of peace.

The prophecies also speak of tumultuous changes happening in the earth, and in our psyche, redefining our relationships and spirituality.

The next *pachacuti,* or great change, has already begun, and it promises the emergence of a new human after this period of turmoil.

To which the Q'ero shamans added in closing:

Follow your own footsteps.
Learn from the rivers,
the trees and the rocks.
Honor the Christ,
the Buddha,
your brothers and sisters.
Honor your Earth Mother and the Great
   Spirit.
Honor yourself and all of creation.
Look with the eyes of your soul and
      engage the essential.

Three timeless civilizations, each a part of the earth's earliest fabric but existing so far from one another, in such remote isolation, that they might as well have lived on different planets. And those ancient civilizations, like too many others to elaborate on here, obviously shared certain common needs that extended far beyond food, clothing and shelter:

*   a need to believe in a Force greater than themselves
*   a need to understand their relationship with the natural world around them
*   a need to formulate prophecies, and

then embrace them as such an essential part of their culture that they passed them like treasured heirlooms from one generation to the next

It may be even more fascinating, though, that those three very separate, isolated societies searched the land, the stars, the rivers, the sun, their own souls, wherever they thought their answers came from, and arrived at prophecies that all added up to the same identical conclusion: humankind's sole hope for sustaining the privilege of life on this earth is through its constant, humble, reverent connection to its own spirituality.

Three remote civilizations, one prophetic conclusion.

It's enough to make you believe those prophecies might all have been coming from the very same Source.

Prophecies and Religion

Without faith, without our beliefs, we're lost. It doesn't matter that God, by whatever name we call Him, never stops believing in us. If we don't reciprocate and keep that connection alive on our end, we're tragically squandering God's belief in us, which is the one gift that makes everything possible. It's like someone calling to announce that you've just won the richest lottery in history—that call is worthless if you don't bother to pick up the phone.

Whether we're consciously aware of it or not, our beliefs are the driving force behind our behavior, our opinions, our actions and in-actions, our decisions and the choices we make. They're essential to our identity, our individuality and, above all, our dialogue with our spirit minds, where our absolute knowledge of our genetic eternity is held for safekeeping. Our beliefs are all we have that can't be taken from us, or threatened or harmed. No matter what specific words and images and allegories we choose to best express and expand those beliefs, they define us, they make each one of us utterly unique because they're ours and ours alone, and yet they unite us all by the breadth and depth of their existence.

The great religions of the world through which we express and explore our beliefs have too much in common to be disrespectful of each other. We all worship a Supreme Being, a loving Creator who gave us the gift of eternal lives. And from the first moments that small groups of followers began to grow into the millions upon millions who practice these great religions today, prophets and prophecies were essential to the story of that growth in each and every case.

Christianity

The temptation is to say, "To see how prophets and prophecies played a part in the dawn of Christianity, read the Holy Bible, pages 1 to 981."

I'm not a fan of hypothetical questions like "Would Christianity have become such a powerful force among world religions without prophets adding so much anticipation to Christ's arrival?" His virgin birth, His unparalleled life, His crucifixion at the age of thirty-three and His resurrection that changed the world forever would certainly have found their way on their own into our hearts and our consciousness on this earth, I'm sure, because I'm certain beyond all doubt that our spirits would have searched until we found Him. But with prophets preparing us for His arrival hundreds of years before He was born, and giving us specifics about how we'd know Him, we were given the added advantage of a divine road map leading straight to Him. Of course I believe that Christ and Christianity were inevitable, according to God's plan, which means I believe that the prophets and their prophecies were inevitable too, along with every other person, event and moment that contributed to Christianity's inception and growth. God is hardly in a position to have to rely on accidents or luck to get His message across, after all.

The Old Testament of the Bible was written between about 1450 B.C. and 430 B.C. It is too rich with prophets—Joseph, Moses, Elisha, Samuel, Hosea, Isaiah, Amos, Ezekiel, Jeremiah, Nathan, Ahijah, Micah, Jonah and Malachi, to name a few—to begin to do it, or its prophecies, even a pathetic attempt at justice, nor would I presume to try for the purposes of this particular discussion.

Instead, I'll focus on only two of the Old Testament prophets whose prophecies were especially descriptive of the life and crucifixion of Christ, which were still hundreds of years in the future, and on Christ's acceptance of His sacred destiny.

The prophet David, king of Israel from approximately 1010 B.C. to 970 B.C., is believed to have written several of the Old Testament's magnificent psalms. Among them is Psalm 22, which contains some prophetic images of Christ's crucifixion too precise to pass by lightly:

My God, my God, why has thou
    forsaken me?
Why art thou so far from helping
    me, from the words of my
    groaning? . . .
In thee our fathers trusted;
    they trusted, and thou didst deliver
      them.
To thee they cried, and were saved;
    in thee they trusted, and were not
      disappointed.
But I am a worm, and no man;
    scorned by men, and despised by
      the people.
All who see me mock at me,
    they make mouths at me, they wag
      their heads;

"He committed his cause to the Lord;
    let him deliver him,
    let him rescue him, for he delights in
        him!". . .
Yea, dogs are round about me;
    a company of evildoers encircle me;
    they have pierced my hands and
        feet—
I can count all my bones—
    they stare and gloat over me;
    they divide my garments among
        them, and for my raiment they cast
        lots . . .

It was hundreds of years later, of course, that Jesus was crucified and the New Testament of the Bible written, probably from 45 A.D. to 95 A.D. One account of the crucifixion, in the New Testament book of Matthew (7:27–50), reads, in part:

Then the soldiers of the governor took Jesus into the praetorium, and they gathered the whole battalion before him. And they stripped him and put a scarlet robe upon him, and plaiting a crown of thorns they put it on his head, and put a reed in his right hand.

And kneeling before him they mocked him, saying, "Hail, King of the Jews!" And they spat upon him, and took the reed and struck him on the head. And when they had mocked him, they stripped him of the robe, and put his own clothes on him, and led him away to crucify him . . .

And when they had crucified him, they divided his garments among them by casting lots; then they sat down and kept watch over him there. And over his head they put the charge against him, which read, "This is Jesus the King of the Jews." . . . And those who passed by derided him, wagging their heads and saying, "You who would destroy the temple and build it in three days, save yourself! If you are the Son of God, come down from the cross." . . . At about the ninth hour Jesus cried with a loud voice, "My God, my God, why hast thou forsaken me?" And some of the bystanders, hearing it, said, "This man is calling Elijah . . . Wait, let us see whether Elijah will come to save him." And Jesus cried again with a loud voice and yielded up his spirit.

The prophet Isaiah, whose book of prophecies appears in the Old Testament, was born in Jerusalem seven hundred years before the birth of Christ. No other prophet was quoted more often than Isaiah by Jesus and His disciples, and it's easy to understand why Isaiah's prophecies about the coming Messiah would have resonated so deeply in the heart of Christ and those who followed Him.

Isaiah 7:14, in the Old Testament, reads, "Therefore the Lord himself will give you a sign. Behold a virgin shall conceive and bear a son and shall call his name Immanuel (which means 'God with us')." And in Matthew 1:18–21, in the New Testament, we find:

Now the birth of Jesus Christ took place in this way. When his mother Mary had been betrothed to Joseph, before they came together she was found to be with child of the Holy Spirit; and her husband Joseph, being a just man and unwilling to put her to shame, resolved to divorce her quietly. But as he considered this, behold, an angel of the Lord appeared to him in a dream, saying, "Joseph, son of David, do not fear to take Mary your wife, for that which is conceived in her is of the Holy Spirit; she will bear a son, and you shall call his name Jesus, for he will save his people from their sins."

From Isaiah 53:3

He was despised and rejected by
*   men;*
a man of sorrows, and acquainted
*   with grief;*
and as one from whom men hide their
*   faces*
he was despised, and we esteemed
*   him not.*

And from the New Testament, Luke 23:13–23

Pilate then called together the chief priests and the rulers and the people, and said to them, "You brought me this man [Jesus] as one who was perverting the people; and after examining him before you, behold, I did not find this man guilty of any of your charges against him; neither did Herod, for he sent him back to us. Behold, nothing deserving death has been done by him; I will therefore chastise him and release him." . . .

But they were urgent, demanding with loud cries that he should be crucified. And their voices prevailed.

Jesus' profound reverence for the prophecies and His divine place among them is woven throughout the New Testament.

In Matthew 5:17, He said, as part of His magnificent Sermon on the Mount, "Think not that I have come to abolish the law and the prophets; I have come not to abolish them but to fulfill them."

In Matthew 26:53–56, as Jesus was captured by a crowd of armed soldiers and high priests and elders in Gethsemane, He said:

"Do you think that I cannot appeal to my Father, and he will at once send me more than twelve legions of angels? But how then should the scriptures be fulfilled, that it must be so?" At that hour Jesus said to the crowds, "Have you come out as against a robber, with swords and clubs to capture me? Day after day I sat in the temple teaching, and you did not seize me. But all this has taken place, that the scriptures of the prophets might be fulfilled."

It's as impossible to cite every prophecy from every prophet in the literature and legacy of Christianity as it is to try to separate the concepts of Christianity and prophecy themselves. They're as intertwined in their historic resonance as they are in their shared sacred Origin.

Judaism

According to the Jewish faith, prophets were far more than simply those who could see the future. They were people chosen by God to speak for Him as His messengers and teachers, and they were admired for their scholarship and their closeness to God.

The greatest of all prophets in Judaism was Moses, who freed the Israelites from their slavery to the Pharaoh and delivered them to the Promised Land of Canaan. It was Moses whom God summoned to the top of the holy mountain of Sinai to present him with the sacred tablets on which the Ten Commandments were written. Jewish faith teaches that Moses saw the combined prophecies of all other prophets to come, so that any prophecies that followed would be nothing more than recitations of what Moses had already seen.

The written Torah, called the Torah Shebiksav, which is God's teaching to the Jewish people, is divided into three parts:

* Torah—the five books presented to Moses by God on Mount Sinai

    Genesis
    Exodus
    Leviticus
    Numbers
    Deuteronomy

* Nevi'im, or Prophets—the messages received by the prophets from God

Joshua
Judges
the two books of Samuel
the two books of Kings
Jeremiah
Ezekiel
Isaiah
Trey Asar, or the Twelve, which
combine the writings of Hosea, Joel,
Amos, Obadiah, Jonah, Micah,
Nahum, Habakkuk, Zephaniah,
Haggai, Zachariah and Malachi

✳ Kesuvim, or Writings—written by the
prophets with God's guidance, but
not devoted exclusively to prophecies

Psalms
Proverbs
Job
Song of Songs
Ruth
Lamentations
Ecclesiastes
Esther
Daniel
Nehemiah
the two books of Chronicles

The Talmud is, to put it *very* basically, the source book of Jewish law, describing how to apply the rules of the Torah to a variety of different circumstances. According to the Talmud, there were actually twice as many prophets as the number of people who fled Egypt. But only the prophets whose messages were intended to apply to future generations were recorded, and those numbered fifty-five—forty-eight males and seven females. The female prophets listed in the Talmud are Sarah, Miriam, Deborah, Hannah, Abigail, Huldah and Esther. Sarah was held in such high esteem as a prophet, in fact, that her ability was thought to be superior to that of her husband, the prophet Abraham.

As I've said in many of my books, I was raised in a Catholic, Lutheran, Presbyterian, Episcopalian, Jewish home. I'm sure that unique upbringing planted the seeds of my lifelong passion for world religions, and I deeply appreciate each of them for the gorgeously singular ways in which they celebrate and glorify God. If I had to credit just one of those influences, though, with my earliest awareness and awe of prophets and their impact in this world, I would give that credit to Judaism.

Islam

Islam is total surrender and obedience to God, called Allah in this religion. Followers of the Islamic faith are called Muslims, and they believe in one God and only one God, our Creator, all-powerful, all-knowing, all-merciful, supreme, sovereign and just. God, or Allah, sent his messengers to guide mankind, and the last of those prophets and messengers was Muhammad. Like all other prophets in Islam, Muhammad was considered to be human and not a part of divinity. Muslims never refer to Muhammad as "Allah." Allah is God and no one else, the only entity in the universe worthy of worship.

Muhammad was born in Makkah (Mecca), in what is now Saudi Arabia, in 570 A.D. Orphaned at a very young age, he was raised by his uncle, Abu Talib, and was recognized early on for his wisdom, honesty, generosity and sincerity. Through his popular gift for arbitrating business disputes, he met a widow named Khadijah, whom he married, and his importance and esteem in Makkah continued to grow.

Never completely comfortable among society, Muhammad went on meditative retreats from time to time, in the cave of Hira, near the "Mountain of Light" not far from Makkah. He was forty years old when, during one of those retreats, the Angel Gabriel appeared to him and delivered the first of what would become twenty-three years' worth of revelations from God. The first revelation read:

Recite: In the name of your Lord who created man from a clot [of blood].
Recite: Your Lord is Most Noble, Who taught by the pen, taught man what he did not know. (96:1–5)

Those twenty-three years of revelations, given to Muhammad by God through the Angel Gabriel, became the miracle of the Qur'an (Koran), the Holy Book of the Islam faith.

Muhammad died at the age of sixty-three. Within a hundred years of his death, Islam had spread throughout Europe and across Asia as far east as China. Muslims cherish and emulate Muhammad as God's final messenger and prophet, but again, their worship is reserved only for God.

One of the most famous of the Islamic prophecies is called "The Final Signs of Qiyaamah [Islam]," their version of the apocalypse:

The ground will cave in:
one in the east,
one in the west,
and one in Hejaz, Saudi Arabia.
Fog or smoke will cover the skies for
*   forty days.*
The nonbelievers will fall conscious,
while Muslims will be ill [develop
*   colds].*
The skies will then clear up.
A night three nights long will follow the
*   fog.*
It will occur in the month of Zil-Hajj*
*   after Eidul-Ahja,***
and cause much restlessness among
*   the people.*
After the night of three nights,
the following morning the sun will rise
*   in the west.*

*People's repentance will not be
   accepted after this incident.
One day later, the Beast from the earth
   will miraculously
emerge from Mount Safaa in Makkah,
   causing a split in the ground.
The beast will be able to talk to people
   and
mark the faces of people,
making the believers' faces glitter, and
the nonbelievers' faces darken.
A breeze from the south causes sores
   in the armpits of Muslims,
which they will die of as a result.
The Ka'aba*** will be destroyed by a
   non-Muslim African group.
Kufr [Godlessness] will be rampant.
Haj [the pilgrimage to Makkah] will be
   discontinued.
The Qur'an will be lifted from the heart
   of the people, thirty years after the
   ruler Muquad's death.
The fire will follow people to Syria,
   after which it will stop.
Some years after the fire,
Qiyaamah [Islam] begins with the Soor
   [trumpet] being blown.
The year is not known to any person.*

*Qiyaamah will come upon the worst of
    creation.*

*(*Zil-Hajj—the last month of the Islamic
    calendar
      **Eidul-Ahja—the Festival of Sacrifice
  ***The Ka'aba—an oblong stone
        building in the center of the Holy
        City of Makkah that houses the
        sacred Black Stone given to
        Abraham by the Angel Gabriel)*

The religion of Islam teaches that because the Bible and the Torah were divinely
revealed by God to their respective
prophets, Christians and Jews deserve the
respect and protection of all Muslims. That
same respect and protection was extended
to Buddhists and Hindus in later years
when the Muslims were conquering parts of
India and realized that, contrary to their first
impressions, the Buddhists and the Hindus
weren't idol-worshippers after all.

In fact, Muslims have a particular respect
for Jesus, and never say His name without
adding the words "peace be upon Him" as
a sign of homage. The Qur'an refers to the
immaculate birth of Christ, acknowledges

His miracles and anticipates His second coming.

Muhammad himself said:

Whoever believes there is no God but Allah, alone without partner, that Muhammad is His messenger, that Jesus is a servant and messenger of God, His worth breathed into Mary and a spirit emanating from Him, and that Paradise and Hell are true, shall be received by God into Heaven.

Respect for other religions besides our own is something a lot of us could learn a lesson or two from, don't you think?

Oh, yes, that, and one other thing—the most frequently spoken word in the language of Islam is "peace."

Buddhism

More than twenty-five hundred years ago a child named Siddhartha Gautama was born in northern India. He would become the Buddha Shakyamuni, "the Enlightened One," and by the beginning of the twenty-first century, 665 million people around the world would be Buddha's devoted followers in a religion and way of life called Buddhism. While there are many different styles of Buddhist practice, some of them basic and simple, some of them very complex, they all maintain the same essential principles from the life and teachings of "the Enlightened One."

According to legend, Queen Maha Maya, wife of King Suddhodana, had a dream one night in which a beautiful white elephant encircled her and entered her right side. Brahmin wise men interpreted the dream to be a sign that a splendid son would be born to the queen and her husband. If that son remained in the palace, he would become a great ruler. If he declined his royal heritage, he would become a Buddha, an Awakened One.

The child was born and named Siddhartha, meaning "All wishes fulfilled." His mother died seven days after his birth, and he was raised with love by his mother's sister, who later married the king. Siddhartha was a brilliant student and athlete, strong, charming, handsome, inquisitive and remarkably compassionate. The king, remembering the words of the Brahmin wise men and not wanting to lose his son to the world outside the palace, created an impossibly exquisite life of privilege and beauty for Prince Siddhartha, while building high guarded walls around the grounds and ordering that his son never be exposed to anything that might disturb his isolated perfection—he should never lay eyes on the seriously ill, the very old, the dying, or certainly not any wandering holy men. The prince married the lovely princess Yasodhara when he was thirteen and lived happily with her in the royal household for thirteen years. But he felt something wasn't right about this life, and the more he stared at those guarded walls around the palace, the more determined he was to know what was beyond them.

He finally began a series of excursions outside the palace walls with the help of his charioteer Channa, and the assault of exposure to the sick, dying, dead and starving devastated him. The belief in India, which was explained to him, was that birth and death are simply an endless cycle that could only be stopped by somehow escaping the trap of continual rebirth. Siddhartha became consumed by the tragic inevitability of birth, deprivation, illness, dying and death over and over again, until his final excursion, when he saw yet another sight he'd never seen before: a small, barefoot man, his head shaved, draped in a simple yellow robe, holding a beggar's bowl. The man's calm face radiated peace and dignity. Channa explained to Siddhartha that the man was a monk, a spiritual man who found happiness in a life of simplicity, purity, discipline and meditation on his journey to be delivered from suffering.

In a decision that would come to be known as the Great Renunciation, Prince Siddhartha left behind his beloved wife and newborn son, his father and stepmother, his royal heritage and unlimited wealth and luxury and, at the age of twenty-nine, set out alone to find a way to end the cycle of suffering and rebirth and then somehow help this sad afflicted world. After six years of pain, severe self-mortification and debilitating discipline, with companions around him who only seemed impressed if he was denying himself even the slightest comfort, he finally concluded that an exhausted, neglected, malnourished body was hardly a welcoming environment for a healthy, awakened, enlightened mind and spirit.

He began to nourish himself again and to rebuild his strength and physical vitality. His companions abandoned him, convinced that he'd given up his disciplines. He was wandering alone in a lovely forest on his thirty-fifth birthday when a woman presented him with a bowl of milk-rice.

"Venerable sir," she said, "whoever you may be, god or human, please accept this offering. May you attain the good which you seek."

Later that day in the same forest he met a groundskeeper who offered him fresh-cut grass for a cushion. Siddhartha laid the cushion of grass at the foot of a spreading fig tree, which later became known as the Bodhi Tree, or "Tree of Enlightenment," and contemplated his life, and his near-death through the futility of his abusively extreme self-discipline.

As he sat beneath the tree he vowed, "Though my skin, my nerves and my lifeblood go dry, I will not abandon this seat until I have realized Supreme Enlightenment."

When he was a young child, Siddhartha

had found himself alone, resting under a tree one day during the Ploughing Festival, and discovered that by sitting cross-legged, eyes closed, mind focused attentively on simply breathing in and out, he could achieve a kind of mental bliss. He had never forgotten that peaceful, private exercise, and he practiced it again that day at the foot of the Bodhi Tree.

A thousand doubts, fears, memories, cravings and temptations assaulted his mind, waging war with all the good he was seeking, as he sat there through a raging storm that thundered during the long night, trying to terrify Siddhartha away from his resolve. But he sat with perfect poise, in meditative serenity, finally asking the Mother Earth Herself for confirmation of the worth of his journey. He reached out with his right hand and touched the ground, and it quaked and trembled and roared back:

"I, Earth, bear you witness!"

And during the night, at different stages of his meditation, he came to know how darkness of the mind is born, and how it is destroyed, never to be born again. He destroyed past, present and future spiritual ignorance. Delusion finally gave way to total clarity, and he finally understood "things as they are."

When dawn came again, Prince Siddhartha had become the great Buddha Shakyamuni, the Enlightened One, and formulated the Four Noble Truths on which all of Buddhism is based:

* that suffering is universal and inevitable
* that the immediate cause of suffering is desire
* that there is a path leading to freedom from suffering
* that it is the Eightfold Path that leads to freedom from suffering

And the Eightfold Path is spelled out as:

* Right (balanced) View or Understanding
* Right Aim or Purpose
* Right Speech
* Right Action
* Right Livelihood
* Right Effort
* Right Mindfulness
* Right Concentration

Buddha gained a great following during his lifetime, expanding on and deepening his teachings and becoming greatly revered throughout the land. He eventually reunited with his father, stepmother, wife and son, all of whom he bestowed with enlightenment and all of whom predeceased him.

Buddha was eighty years old when he died, surrounded by teachers who had learned at his feet and would carry on his message. He didn't name a successor. Ancient texts say that as he entered a final state of meditative bliss and passed away, the trees around him blossomed out of season and fragrant flowers scattered to encircle his body in homage.

One of the many gorgeous aspects of Buddhism, clearly inspired by the life of Buddha himself, is that it's an active, self-propelled religion. Buddha's enlightenment was the result of his own determined efforts, and Buddhists are taught that the same is true of their own enlightenment, its depth and its benefits—they're the sole responsibility of each individual's efforts and no one else's. If something is missing from your life, don't look to Buddha, or to the people around you, in other words. Look to yourself.

The Buddhist scripts contain a prophecy of another Buddha, a future Buddha still to come. He currently resides in the *Tutshita,* or heaven, and his next incarnation will be his last. His name, the scripture says, will be Maitreya, "the Best of Men":

He will have a heavenly voice which reaches far; his skin will have a golden hue; a great splendor will radiate from his body; his chest will be broad, limbs well developed, and his eyes will be like lotus petals. His body is eighty cubits high, and twenty cubits broad. He will have a retinue of eighty-four thousand persons, whom he will instruct in the mantras. With this retinue he will one day go forth into the homeless life. A Dragon tree will then be the tree under which he will win enlightenment; its branches rise up to fifty leagues, and its foliage spreads far and wide over six Kos. Underneath it, Maitreya, the best of men, will attain enlightenment; there can be no doubt on that. And he will win his enlightenment the very same day that he has gone forth into the homeless life. And then, a supreme sage, he will explain the Four Truths, because he has seen that generation, in faith, ready for them, and those who have listened to his Dharma [means of protecting ourselves from ignorance] will thereupon make progress. They will be assembled in a park full of beautiful flowers, and his assembly will extend over a hundred leagues. Under Maitreya's guidance, hundreds of thousands of living beings shall enter upon a religious life.

Hinduism

The third largest religion in the world is Hinduism, thought to have followers numbering well over 750 million. Its roots are deeply imbedded in the Indus valley of northern India, but the beliefs about how and when those roots were planted seem to be a matter of debate. One school of thought takes Hinduism back to somewhere between 4000 B.C. and 2200 B.C. and the influence of the Indo-European invaders, who practiced a religion called Vedism. Another is that the Indo-European invasion may never have happened at all and that the Hindu religious texts were the result of an already sophisticated Vedic culture in India.

There's no disagreement, though, that this ancient religion, unlike the others we've discussed, wasn't the result of any one leader or group of leaders, or any one prophet or group of prophets, or any specific sequence of events. Hinduism seems to have *evolved* instead, although its sacred texts can certainly be narrowed down a little better than that. Those texts include "the Vedas," four volumes containing hymns, incantations and rituals from ancient India, which were committed to paper around 600 B.C., and "the Upanishads," which expanded on the Vedic philosophy and were written between 800 B.C. and 400 B.C.

Hinduism recognizes one supreme God, the principle of "Brahman," one divine entity who is both at one with the universe and transcends it at the same time. Brahman, though, is believed to exist as three separate parts:

✴ Brahma, the Creator, who perpetually creates new realities
✴ Vishnu, or Krishna, the Preserver, the

protector and preserver of the creations; when eternal order is threatened, it's Vishnu who travels to earth, in the form of any of ten incarnations he chooses

* Shiva, the Destroyer

Hindus believe that everything comes from nothing and goes back to nothing, in cycle after cycle. Therefore Brahma creates the universe, Vishnu takes over as its caretaker and then Shiva destroys it so that Brahma can begin the cycle again. The cycles are very long, with current Hindu wisdom suggesting that the universe has approximately 427,000 years left before this one ends and a new cycle begins.

Hindus gear their lives toward what they call the "four aims of Hinduism." Three of those aims are the goals of those who are in the world, or the *pravritti*:

* *dharma:* righteousness in their religious life
* *artha:* economic success and material prosperity
* *kama:* finding sensual, sexual and mental enjoyment

The fourth aim is for the *nivritti,* or those who renounce the world:

✱ *moksa:* liberation from *samsara,* the indefinitely repeated cycles of karma involved in the Hindu's interpretation of reincarnation and eternity

The Hindu faith embraces the concept that our bodies die, but our souls are eternal. When the soul leaves the body at the time of death, it simply passes on to another body. That next body can be human or any other living thing, depending on the kind and quality of life lived in the previous body, and the continuing cycle of birth, life, death and rebirth is called *samsara.* By the Hindu definition, karma is the net total of one's good deeds and bad deeds throughout a lifetime. Karma in one lifetime determines how you'll live your next one— whether you'll be reborn at a higher level, perhaps as a more successful, wealthier or more privileged person, or at a lower level, perhaps as a severely disadvantaged person or even the most humble of animals. Eventually, through the purest of acts, thoughts and total commitment to God, the soul can escape samsara and achieve true enlightenment.

And to the Hindu, the ultimate goal has nothing to do with heaven, or status and admiration among others in the faith. The ultimate goal is simply to be in selfless service of God, in whatever highest, purest ways the individual can find for that service to express itself.

Because Hinduism is such an ancient religion, there are many divisions and variations in customs, traditions and details. Hindus are not unlike Catholics, Presbyterians, Methodists, et al., all appropriately falling under the much larger heading of Christianity. Hindu sects are enormously tolerant of each other, and of other religions for that matter, believing as they do that there are many paths to the one true omnipotent God.

The Hindu Puranas, which are a written weaving of mythology and history, contain a list of Hindu prophecies. I saved them for last in this chapter because I have a feeling you'll want to read several of them more than once.

  ✳ Apocalypse for the Hindu is the natural ending of the world in the fourth age, the Kali Age [Age of Darkness and Discord].

* It is one of a series of apocalypses, each of which marks the end of one cycle and the beginning of another creation. The central figure in the story is Vishnu, the preserver God, into whose self the world is absorbed before being born again.

* Vishnu has already saved humanity on a number of occasions, symbolically appearing as a savior in many different forms. It is said that He will appear again soon, as Kalki, a white horse, destined to destroy the present world and to take humanity to a different, higher plane.

* All kings occupying the earth in the Kali Age will be wanting in tranquillity, strong in anger, taking pleasure at all times in lying and dishonesty, inflicting death on women, children and cows, prone to take the paltry possessions of others, with character that is mostly vile, rising to power and soon falling.

* They will be short-lived, ambitious, of little virtue and greedy. People will follow the customs of others and be

adulterated with them; peculiar, un-
disciplined barbarians will be vigor-
ously supported by rulers. Because
they go on living with perversion, they
will be ruined.

* Dharma [eternal order, righteousness]
becomes very weak in the Kali Age.
People commit sin in mind, speech
and actions.

* Quarrels, plague, fatal diseases,
famines, drought and calamities appear. Testimonies and proofs have no
certainty. There is no criterion left
when the Kali Age settles down.

* People become poorer in vigor and
luster.

* They are wicked, full of anger, sinful,
false and avaricious.

* Bad ambitions, bad education, bad
dealings and bad earnings excite fear.

* The whole batch becomes greedy
and untruthful.

* Many sudras [Godless ones] will become kings, and many heretics will be
seen.

* There will arise various sects; san-
nyasins [elevated ones, gurus] wearing clothes colored red.

* Many profess to have supreme knowledge because, thereby, they will easily earn their livelihood.
* In the Kali Age, there will be many false religionists.
* India will become desolate by repeated calamities, short lives and various diseases.
* Everyone will be miserable owing to the dominance of vice and Tamoguna [apathy, inaction].
* Earth will be valued only for her mineral treasures.
* Money alone will confer nobility.
* Power will be the sole definition of virtue.
* Pleasure will be the only reason for marriage.
* Lust will be the only reason for womanhood.
* Falsehood will win out in disputes.
* Being dry of water will be the only definition of land.
* Praiseworthiness will be measured by accumulated wealth.
* Propriety will be considered good conduct, and only feebleness will be the reason for unemployment.

* Boldness and arrogance will be equivalent to scholarship.
* Only those without wealth will show honesty.
* Just a bath will amount to purification, and charity will be the only virtue.
* Abduction will be marriage.
* Simply to be well dressed will signify propriety.
* Any hard-to-reach water will be deemed a pilgrimage site.
* The pretense of greatness will be the proof of it, and powerful men with many severe faults will rule over all the classes on earth.
* Oppressed by their excessively greedy rulers, people will hide in valleys between mountains, where they will gather honey, vegetables, roots, fruits, birds, flowers and so forth.
* Suffering from cold, wind, heat and rain, they will put on clothes made of tree bark and leaves.
* And no one will live as long as twenty-three years.
* Thus in the Kali Age humankind will be utterly destroyed.

CHAPTER TWO

*

What Is a Prophet?

"I do not know whether it is owing to the anxiety of my mind, or what, but this afternoon, as I was sitting at this table engaged in preparing a dispatch, something seemed to disturb me. Looking up, I beheld standing opposite me a singularly beautiful female. So astonished was I, for I had given strict orders not to be disturbed, that it was some moments before I found language to inquire the cause of her presence. A second, a third and even a fourth time did I repeat my question, but received no answer from my mysterious visitor except a slight raising of her eyes.

"By this time I felt strange sensations

spreading through me. I would have risen but the riveted gaze of the being before me rendered volition impossible. I assayed once more to address her, but my tongue had become useless, as though it had become paralyzed.

"A new influence, mysterious, potent, irresistible, took possession of me. All I could do was to gaze steadily, vacantly at my unknown visitor. Gradually the surrounding atmosphere seemed as if it had become filled with sensations, and luminous. Everything about me seemed to rarify, the mysterious visitor herself becoming more airy and yet more distinct to my sight than before. I now began to feel as one dying, or rather to experience the sensations which I have sometimes imagined accompany dissolution. I did not think, I did not reason, I did not move; all were alike impossible. I was only conscious of gazing fixedly, vacantly at my companion.

"Presently I heard a voice saying, 'Son of the Republic, look and learn,' while at the same time my visitor extended her arm eastwardly. I now beheld a heavy white vapor at some distance rising fold upon fold. This gradually dissipated, and I looked upon a strange scene. Before me lay spread out in one vast plain all the countries of the world: Europe, Asia, Africa and America. I saw rolling and tossing between Europe and America the billows of the Atlantic, and between Asia and America lay the Pacific.

" 'Son of the Republic,' said the same mysterious voice as before, 'look and learn.' At that moment I beheld a dark, shadowy being, like an angel, standing, or rather floating in midair, between Europe and America. Dipping water out of the ocean in the hollow of each hand, he sprinkled some upon America with his right hand, while with his left hand he cast some on Europe. Immediately a cloud raised from these countries, and joined in mid-ocean. For a while it remained stationary, and then moved slowly westward, until it enveloped America in its murky folds. Sharp flashes of lightning gleamed through it at intervals, and I heard the smothered groans and cries of the American people.

"A second time the angel dipped water from the ocean, and sprinkled it out as before. The dark cloud was then drawn back to the ocean, in whose heaving billows it sank from view. A third time I heard the mysterious voice saying, 'Son of the Republic, look and learn.' I cast my eyes upon America and beheld villages and towns and cities springing up one after another until the whole land from the Atlantic to the Pacific was dotted with them.

"Again, I heard the mysterious voice say, 'Son of the Republic, the end of the century cometh, look and learn.' At this the dark shadowy angel turned his face southward, and from Africa I saw an ill-omened specter approach our land. It flitted slowly over every town and city of the latter. The inhabitants presently set themselves in battle array against each other. As I continued looking I saw a bright angel, on whose brow rested a crown of light, on which was traced the word 'Union,' bearing the American flag which he placed between the divided nation, and said, 'Remember ye are brethren.' Instantly, the inhabitants, casting from them their weapons, became friends once more, and united around the National Standard.

"And again I heard the mysterious voice saying, 'Son of the Republic, look and learn.' At this the dark, shadowy angel placed a trumpet to his mouth, and blew three distinct blasts, and taking water from the ocean, he sprinkled it upon Europe, Asia and Africa. Then my eyes beheld a fearful scene: from each of these countries arose thick, black clouds that were soon joined into one. Throughout this mass there gleamed a dark red light by which I saw hordes of armed men, who, moving with the cloud, marched by land and sailed by sea to America. Our country was enveloped in this volume of cloud, and I saw these vast armies devastate the whole country and burn the villages, towns and cities that I beheld springing up. As my ears listened to the thundering of the cannon, clashing of swords, and the shouts and cries of millions in mortal combat, I heard again the mysterious voice saying, 'Son of the Republic, look and learn.' When the voice had ceased, the dark shadowy angel placed his trumpet once more to his mouth, and blew a long and fearful blast.

"Instantly a light as of a thousand suns shone down from above me, and pierced and broke into fragments the dark cloud which enveloped America. At the same moment the angel upon whose head still shone the word 'Union,' and who bore our national flag in one hand and a sword in the other, descended from the heavens attended by legions of white spirits. These immediately joined the inhabitants of America, who I perceived were well nigh overcome, but who, immediately taking courage again, closed up their broken ranks and renewed the battle.

"Again, amid the fearful noise of the conflict, I heard the mysterious voice saying, 'Son of the Republic, look and learn.' As the voice ceased, the shadowy angel for the last time dipped water from the ocean and sprinkled it upon America. Instantly the dark cloud rolled back, together with the armies it had brought, leaving the inhabitants of the land victorious!

"Then once more I beheld the villages, towns and cities springing up where I had seen them before, while the bright angel, planting the azure standard he had brought in the midst of them, cried with a loud voice, 'While the stars remain, and the heavens send down dew upon the earth, so long shall the Union last.' And taking from his brow the crown on which blazoned the word 'Union,' he placed it upon the Standard while the people, kneeling down, said, 'Amen.'

"The scene instantly began to fade and dissolve, and I at last saw nothing but the rising, curling vapor I at first beheld. This also disappearing, I found myself once more gazing upon the mysterious visitor, who, in the same voice I had heard before, said, 'Son of the Republic, what you have seen is thus interpreted: three great perils will come upon the Republic. The most fearful is the third, but in this greatest conflict the whole world united shall not prevail against her. Let every child of the Republic learn to live for his God, his land and the Union. With these words the vision vanished, and I started from my seat and felt that I had seen a vision wherein had been shown to me the birth, progress and destiny of the United States."

If that quote isn't familiar to you, I'm sure you're wondering the same thing I did the first time I saw it: what American prophet should I have been paying more attention to?

And you might be as surprised as I was to hear that what you've just read was written in 1777, not by some mysterious, cloak-draped spiritualist or trance medium or fortune-teller but by our first president, George Washington.

I think one of the things I least expected when I started actively studying prophets and prophecies in my early twenties was how diverse and unique each of them was. I've long since forgotten what my predisposed image of a typical prophet might have been before then. I'm sure it was a little otherworldly, not living in ordinary houses having ordinary problems and ordinary friends and families and ordinary jobs and, God forbid, even ordinary, mundane conversations, but instead kind of wafting around like a virtual hermit, spouting prophecies when not busy meditating. As it turns out, prophets—or maybe "those who were prophetic" puts it in better perspective, since it's rarely a full-time career—are much more interesting than I ever dreamed they'd be, precisely because there is no such thing as a "typical prophet"; they're actually just an extraordinary array of people who happened to be able to peer into and express the near and the distant future.

It would be ludicrous for me to imply that

I can cover every significant prophet and prophecy in one book, let alone one chapter. All I hope to accomplish in this chapter is to share some glimpses of a few of the prophets and prophecies that have made lasting impressions on me. If it inspires you to explore further, great. If it does nothing more than help you take a slightly different view of the word "prophet" than you might have had when you opened this book, I'll be happy.

For example, here's a quote that's likely to seem very familiar to you:

Like anybody, I would like to live a long life. Longevity has its place. But I'm not concerned about that now. I just want to do God's will. And He's allowed me to go up to the mountain. And I've looked over. And I've seen the promised land. I may not get there with you. But I want you to know tonight that we, as a people, will get to the promised land. And I'm happy tonight. I'm not worried about anything. I'm not fearing any man. Mine eyes have seen the glory of the coming of the Lord.

That, of course, was the conclusion of the magnificent sermon delivered at the Masonic Temple in Memphis, Tennessee, by Dr. Martin Luther King, Jr., on the night of April 3, 1968. In the late afternoon of April 4, less than twenty-four hours later, Dr. King was assassinated, and the world lost a great, courageous, passionate friend.

In any context, that sermon in Memphis in 1968 remains one of the most eloquent speeches in American history.

But in the context of Dr. King's imminent death, it's so movingly prophetic that I'd be doing him an outrageous disservice if I didn't include him in a chapter about some of the prophets who've passed our way.

Also passing our way was Abraham Lincoln, who, in November of 1864, three and a half years after the Civil War began, wrote the following in a letter to Colonel William F. Elkins:

I see in the near future a crisis approaching that unnerves me and causes me to tremble for the safety of my country. As a result of the war, corporations have been enthroned, and an era of corruption in high places will follow, and the money power of the country will endeavor to prolong its reign by working upon the prejudices of the people until all wealth is aggregated in a few hands and the Republic is destroyed. I feel at this moment more anxiety for the safety of my country than ever before, even in the midst of war.

Don't you wish he could come back today, spend a week or so in Washington, D.C., just listening and observing, and go on national TV to give us *his* version of a State of the Union address?

And then there was Sir Winston Churchill, former prime minister of England, Nobel Prize winner, unparalleled statesman and orator and achiever of enough other accomplishments during his lifetime that his gift of prophecy tends to get overshadowed. To name just a handful of Churchill's traceable, recorded prophecies, he predicted:

* the German invasion of France, two years before it happened
* the atomic bomb

* the formal establishment of the state of Israel
* the gathering evil of Adolf Hitler, years before the rest of the world caught on
* the German invasion of Russia, despite the pact between Hitler and Stalin
* the fierce aggression of the Soviet Union under Stalin against Europe
* the ultimate demise of any "criminals" who assaulted innocent civilian populations by air, even during war, several months before Germany unleashed the devastating "Blitzkrieg" bombing of London
* the collapse of the Soviet Union

In fact, Churchill had such an impressive accuracy rate as a prophet that it makes me wonder how some of our leaders can so arrogantly ignore another of his clear and simple warnings:

If you go on with this nuclear arms race, all you are going to do is make the rubble bounce.

Nostradamus

Probably when you hear the word "prophet" you're likely to think of Nostradamus, who's without question one of the most famous, most prolific, most exhaustively written about and most tirelessly debated prophets in history. One school of thought on Nostradamus is that we've only begun to scratch the surface of the brilliance of his prophecies. Another is that the language of his prophecies is so vague and obscure that they could be interpreted as predictions of almost anything. Still another is that it all depends on the accuracy of the translations, since Nostradamus's prophecies were originally written in French in the 1500s, with some Greek, Latin and word puzzles thrown in for good measure. Which means as far as I'm concerned that whether he was a genuinely gifted prophet or an ingenious fraud, he's held our interest for almost half a millennium, so it's impossible to argue with his remarkable impact.

He was born Michel de Nostradame in St. Remy de Provence, France, in 1503. The family lineage was Jewish, but they had converted to Christianity and raised Michel in the Catholic faith. After putting in his years as a talented student, he graduated from the University of Montpellier and became an equally talented physician.

A deadly plague ravaged France a few years into Nostradamus's medical career, and patient after patient not only survived but recovered completely for no other reason than being in his remarkably successful care. He was also accused of heresy, and of being a magician (a serious charge under the circumstances) for his seemingly suspicious ability to cure the incurable, but his battle against the terrible illness had earned him enough renown that the Pope himself protected him against the charges. In one of those twists of fate that almost seem too cruel to be true, Nostradamus became a hero for treating the same plague that ended up killing his beloved wife and two children.

Their deaths devastated him, and he seems to have been fairly aimless for the next six years, traveling throughout France and Italy. It was during these years of grieving and struggling to heal his broken heart that he first felt the prophetic gift inside him starting to wake up. According to one of countless stories from those six years, Nostradamus encountered a group of Franciscan monks on a path in Italy. Like any good, respectful Catholic, he was in the process of stepping aside to get out of their way when suddenly, for no apparent reason, he was overcome with awe, fell to his knees and genuflected, reaching to reverently touch the robe of Father Felice Peretti, the least distinguished and most lowly born monk in the group.

"What are you doing?" the monk asked him. "Why are you behaving like this?"

To which Nostradamus replied, "I must yield myself and bow before his Holiness."

Nostradamus died in 1566. In 1585 Felice Peretti became Pope Sixtus V.

Nostradamus eventually remarried and made a home for himself and his wife Anne Ponsart Gemelle in Salon, France. It was in Salon that he started a new family, which ultimately totaled six children. And it was also in Salon that he started his prophetic writings.

The structure of Nostradamus's writing as a prophet is very distinctive. First, he wrote in four-line verses called quatrains. Then he organized the quatrains into what he called "Centuries"—one hundred quatrains per Century, theoretically, although since he wrote a total of 942 quatrains in his lifetime, there was one Century that only contained forty-two quatrains.

Nostradamus was fifty-two years old when he wrote his first quatrains. It's a tribute to his continued fame and brilliant reputation in the medical world, and the quickly spreading word of his gifts as a prophet, that nine years later he was appointed royal physician to King Charles IX.

Legend has it that on July 1, 1566, Nostradamus had spent time with his priest and was in the process of leaving when the priest said as a casual good-bye, "Until tomorrow."

Nostradamus turned, looked at him and stated with calm, quiet authority, "You will not find me alive at sunrise."

And that night, at the age of sixty-three, Nostradamus died.

Again, the answer to "What exactly did he predict?" depends on which camp of the ongoing controversy you talk to. "Anything you want to read into him" will be one answer. "Who can tell, with all that Greek and

Latin and all those anagrams thrown in, and translators who may not have been accurate in the first place?" will be another answer.

But for those who believe the answer is "Almost every significant world event since the 1600s," the list of Nostradamus's accurate prophecies is almost endless, far too exhaustive to do justice to here, and even now, in 2004, many of them still lie ahead of us, waiting to unfold.

Among the most often quoted, especially in recent years, involve his warnings of three powerful, tyrannical, sadistic Antichrists who would terrorize, brutalize and demand slavish loyalty from his own people.

His description of the first of these Antichrists has been translated to read:

An Emperor shall be born near Italy
Who shall cost the Empire dear,
They shall say, with what people he
*   keeps company*
He shall be found less a Prince than a
*   butcher . . .*
From a simple soldier he will rise to the
*   Empire,*

*From the short robe he will attain the
  long.
Great swarms of bees shall arise.*

This is unanimously thought to be a description of Napoleon, the emperor of France from 1799 to 1814. He was born on the island of Corsica, fifty miles from the coast of Italy, in 1769. No one would argue the description of "butcher." And for his imperial crest, he chose the symbol of the beehive.

The next Antichrist of Nostradamus's prophecies would be a "great enemy of the human race" and a master manipulator:

*Out of the deepest part of the west of
  Europe,
From poor people a young child shall
  be born,
Who with his tongue shall seduce
  many people,
His fame shall increase in the Eastern
  Kingdom.
He shall come to tyrannize the land.
He shall raise up a hatred that had long
  been dormant.
The child of Germany observes no law.
Cries, and tears, fire, blood, and battle.*

This has obviously been widely accepted as a description of Adolf Hitler, born into a poor family in Austria in 1889. And to say he "tyrannized" and "raised up a hatred" and "observed no law" after "seducing many people with his tongue" is to soft-pedal what a vicious, psychopathic, inhuman monster that "child of Germany" really was.

The third Antichrist is a great subject of current interest, for reasons that will be obvious the minute you start reading Nostradamus's description:

Out of the country of Greater Arabia
Shall be born a strong master of
    Muhammad . . .
He will enter Europe wearing a blue
    turban.
He will be the terror of mankind . . .

From the sky will come the great King
    of Terror.
He will bring back to life the King of the
    Mongols;
Before and after war reigns.

The sky will burn at forty-five degrees.
Fire approaches the great new city.

By fire he will destroy their city,
A cold and cruel heart,
Blood will pour,
Mercy to none.

By the way, this brings up a perfect example of how different scholars can interpret the same passages in different ways and still come up with the same answer. It's always been widely accepted that the "great new city" was a reference to New York City. Before September 11, 2001, the words "the sky will burn at forty-five degrees" were taken as an "obvious" indication of New York's location near forty-five degrees latitude. After September 11, 2001, those words became an "obvious" image of the World Trade Center, consumed in flames from that unspeakable act of terrorism, burning so high in the air before the towers collapsed that the flames were at a forty-five degree angle to the horizon.

God bless New York, though, and sorry, Nostradamus, but even after taking the most horrific sucker punch on its own soil in this country's history, that city was most certainly *not* destroyed.

As for the identity of that third Antichrist, you'll find those who swear it's Saddam Hussein, and those who use the description of the attack on the World Trade Center to point out how clear it is that it's Osama bin Laden. I'll keep my opinion on that to myself, except to add a plea of my own inspired by these passages:

To use such words of Nostradamus's as "out of the country of Greater Arabia" and "a master of Muhammad" and "wearing a turban" as an excuse for discriminating against Middle Easterners and/or committing hate crimes against them as retribution for the despicable acts of "one of their own" is exactly as insane, as far as I'm concerned, as holding all of us who happen to be Caucasian accountable for the acts of our fellow Caucasians Napoleon and Hitler.

So let's save our outrage for its most specific, appropriate targets, shall we, unless we want to wake up one day on the receiving end of a whole lot of misplaced outrage ourselves?

Sir Arthur Conan Doyle

If Arthur Conan Doyle had accomplished nothing in his lifetime but create the legendary detective Sherlock Holmes, and then feature him in four novels and fifty-six short stories, he'd have more than earned our attention.

If he'd limited himself to his successful career as a physician and surgeon, he would have had a full, rewarding life. That career included service in a medical unit in South Africa, which led to his writing an article called "The War in South Africa: Its Causes and Conduct" in defense of England's handling of the Boer War and its aftermath. He was knighted by King Edward VII for that article, an honor he would have modestly declined if his mother hadn't convinced him to accept.

His personal life alone would have been enough to keep most men too confused to accomplish much of anything. He met his wife Louise when he treated her brother Jack for terminal cerebral meningitis. Jack's illness and death drew them into a marriage of enormous fondness and respect, and they had two children together as Conan Doyle made the transition from his life as a doctor to his brilliant literary career. When Louise was diagnosed with tuberculosis in 1893, Conan Doyle moved his family to healthier climates in an effort to help her, eventually ending up in Hindshead, Surrey, England, in 1897, where he met and fell instantly in love with a woman named Jean Leckie. For nearly the next ten years, Arthur Conan Doyle and Jean Leckie carried on a deeply passionate but purely platonic relationship, Conan Doyle somehow never violating his oath that Louise was never to know about Jean and was never, ever to be hurt. When Louise died in 1906, Conan Doyle sank into health problems and depression for a while, until he'd recovered from the guilt and the pressure of so much secret-keeping and withholding from a wife who'd devoted her life to him, and he and Jean were finally married in the fall of 1907.

The fact that Conan Doyle found time to develop even a passing interest in spiritualism is amazing under the circumstances. But he did far more than that. Sir Arthur Conan Doyle ultimately devoted the full force of his attention and reputation to the world of spiritualism. He was raised in a devoutly Catholic home but became an agnostic and showed no interest in any belief system until he attended a lecture on spiritualism in 1881. Some facet of it clearly resonated in him, since from then on he attended séances, began writing articles for spiritualist publications, volunteered to be hypnotized at a lecture on mesmerism and, in 1893, joined the British Society for Psychical Research, an organization that, among other things, investigated alleged hauntings and similar unexplained phenomena. By 1920 Conan Doyle was one of England and America's most active and courageous writers and public speakers on the subjects of spiritualism and the afterlife. He knew it would cost him some of the credibility he'd spent a lifetime earning, and it did. But he was so sure of his spiritualist convictions that he paid that price with no apologies until the day he died in 1930.

It's no big surprise that a man as openminded, diverse and spiritually available as Sir Arthur Conan Doyle would find himself in possession of prophecies that he felt compelled to express out of his lifelong concern for humankind. Between information he channeled from his Spirit Guide Phineas and material he gathered from mediums he'd come to know and respect throughout England and the United States, Conan Doyle wrote a letter shortly before his death that spelled out the prophecies he'd been given to pass along to anyone who cared to pay attention. The letter, published in July of 1930, predicted:

* A period of natural convulsions during which a large portion of the human race will perish; earthquakes of great severity and enormous tidal waves would seem to be the agents.
* War appears only in the early stages and appears to be a signal for the crisis to follow; the crisis will come in an instant.
* The destruction and dislocation of civilized life will be beyond belief.
* There will be a short period of chaos followed by some reconstruction; the total period of upheavals will be roughly three years.
* The chief centers of disturbance will be the Eastern Mediterranean basin,

where not less than five countries will entirely disappear.

* Also in the Atlantic there will be a rise of land which will be a cause of those waves which will bring about great disasters upon the Americas, the Irish and Western European shore, involving all of the low-lying British coasts.

* There are indicated further great upheavals in the southern Pacific and in the Japanese region.

* Mankind can be saved by returning to its spiritual values.

Madame Helena Blavatsky

Like the other prophets in this chapter, Madame Blavatsky and her complicated, fascinating life can't be done any real justice in a few short pages, but I'd love to think you'll be intrigued enough by what you read here to explore further. Believe me, you won't be disappointed or bored. Helena Petrovna Blavatsky was an extraordinary woman, as outspoken as she was controversial. I won't promise that you'll find her own writings enjoyable. In fact, they can be a lot of work—dense, obtuse and a struggle to get through. But a biography, or a few studies of her exhaustive work in the fields of religion, philosophy and the occult, would be valuable additions to your library.

Helena Blavatsky was born in Russia in 1831. Her father was a soldier in the Russian army, and her mother was a successful novelist. One of the first of countless peculiarities about her life is that she often claimed that her mother died when she was an infant, when the truth is that she was twelve when her mother died. She wasn't an especially healthy, stable child, and there are accounts of her sleepwalking at a very early age and of occasional emotionally triggered convulsions.

The Russian culture into which Helena Blavatsky was born was an almost devoutly superstitious one, and little Helena was fascinated with the talk of otherworldly beings and powers that were a common part of the tapestry of her childhood. The willow trees by the river where her nurses took her for walks, for example, were said to be populated by green-haired nymphs called *russalkas.* One day when Helena was four, a fourteen-year-old boy began teasing her during a walk with her nurse, and she angrily let out a roar and threatened to have the *russalkas* tickle him to death. He was frightened enough to run away from her, disappearing over the riverbank. He wasn't seen again until weeks later, when his drowned, lifeless body washed up on the shore downstream. There are any number of logical explanations for what was undoubtedly an accidental death. But in later years Helena would refer to the homicide she committed at the age of four.

Apparently none of her nurses or other servants in the household were sure enough of themselves to argue the point, because they secretly performed rituals centered around their belief that little Helena was special and powerful and could control supernatural beings. She decided they were probably right, she *was* special and powerful, and a well-placed, full-blown temper tantrum when she didn't get her way certainly did seem to satisfy her need for control over everyone in the household, supernatural or not. Her family tried everything from scoldings to corporal punishment to exorcisms, but this child wasn't about to modify any behavior that ultimately suited her purposes.

When Helena's mother died, she and her two siblings went to live with their maternal grandparents. Helena's grandmother was a renowned botanist, and it's no stretch of psychology to say that a very headstrong, extremely self-confident young girl, raised by first a mother and then a grandmother who commanded and received respect for their hard-won careers, wasn't being shaped for a quiet, dutiful life as a housewife in the mid-1800s Russian version of suburbia.

The first real love affair Helena claimed was with Prince Alexander Galistin. She was sixteen, and she was probably more attracted to his interest in the occult than she was to him. When she was seventeen she embarked on what was by all accounts a loveless marriage to General Nicephore Blavatsky, who was more than twice her age. She left him after three months, actually escaping past his bodyguards to get away, and spent the next ten years in a haze of travel, the details of which vary from one biography to another. Her version included two years in Tibet, studying with the

Lama, and a story that her fans claim was a pivotal experience in her life as a medium and her critics claim never happened.

She was in India in 1856, she said, when, wearing a disguise, she gained entry to an amazing reincarnation ceremony by showing the guard a special talisman she'd carried with her since childhood.

The ceremony itself began with a four-month-old baby being laid on a long prayer rug or carpet in the center of the small assembled group. Then, according to Helena Blavatsky's account:

Under the influence of the venerable lama, the baby rose to its feet and walked up and down the strip of carpet, repeating, 'I am Buddha, I am the old Lama, I am his spirit in a new body.'

Whatever can be made of Helena Blavatsky's story, there seems to be no question that she did spend time in Tibet, where admittance was not granted easily in the 1800s, particularly to women.

Helena finally returned to Russia and to Blavatsky, on the condition that she be required to spend as little time with him as possible. She began holding séances in her grandfather's home, frequently attended by two of her cousins and a cross-section of highly educated Russian intellectuals who were becoming increasingly intrigued by the paranormal in general and by Madame Blavatsky in particular. A guest at several of the séances later wrote, "On one occasion she caused a closed piano in an adjacent room to emit sounds as if invisible hands were playing upon it. This was done in my presence, at the insistence of one of the guests."

Helena Blavatsky's appeal obviously wasn't limited to her paranormal gifts, since somehow in the next few years she found herself romantically involved with both an Estonian spiritualist named Nicholas Meyendorff and a married opera singer named Agardi Metrovich, all while continuing to live with her husband and hold regular séances in her grandfather's parlor. The most conspicuous consequence of this impossibly complicated period of her life was the birth of a child, a boy named Yuri, who was born deformed. None of the men Helena was involved with claimed paternity of him, and the specifics of his deformities have never been completely clear. But when

Yuri was five years old, Helena took him to Spain to get him some kind of medical attention. Tragically, Yuri didn't survive the trip, and Helena lovingly brought her son back to Russia to bury him in his homeland.

Her child's life and death had an enormous impact on her. She later wrote in a letter that "I loved one man deeply but still more I love occult science," and yet nothing else "in all the world" would ever surpass her love for Yuri. In a separate letter she also wrote that the Russian Orthodox God had died for her on the day of Yuri's death. She never quite abandoned her religious beliefs completely, though, and also wrote that "there were moments when I believed deeply . . . that the blood of Christ has redeemed me."

Money was dwindling, and Helena's life as a medium and her passion for the occult demanded more fertile ground and inspiration than she could find around her anymore. She began to travel, to Odessa, to Egypt and to Paris, and it was in Paris that she heard about the spiritualist movement that was taking root in the United States. She saw it as a new beginning and, almost without a dime to her name, boarded a steamship to cross the Atlantic, arriving in New York in July of 1873.

She struggled along, barely making ends meet, holding séances on Sunday nights and working in sweatshops when she could, until finally, one day in October 1874, she made her way to a remote farm in Chittenden, Vermont, for the purpose of introducing herself to Colonel Henry Steele Olcott.

Colonel Olcott, a former appointee to a three-man commission to investigate the assassination of President Lincoln, had been hired by the *New York Daily Graphic* to write a series of research articles on the Eddy Brothers, who were conducting séances at the Chittenden farm. Helena had read the first of those articles when she decided that Colonel Olcott was someone she wanted and needed to meet.

She stayed for ten days, conducting séances along with the Eddy Brothers. While Colonel Olcott wasn't an avowed spiritualist, he was certainly interested in the paranormal as a journalist and a researcher, and he was very impressed with the exotic Madame Blavatsky. He wrote several articles about her, and he was delighted when she volunteered to translate them for publication in Russia.

What followed was yet another rocky, difficult, sometimes contentious period in Helena's life. But her fame throughout New York and beyond began to spread, and her relationship with Colonel Olcott ultimately blossomed into the founding of the Theosophical Society in September 1875. It's a credit to Helena Blavatsky and Colonel Henry Olcott that the Theosophical Society is still alive and well in 2004. It was basically formed to study spiritualism, the occult sciences, Egyptian mysteries, the kabbalah and other related esoteric fields. It was, and is, a nondenominational, nondogmatic organization devoted to cultural understanding between Eastern and Western philosophies, religions and sciences. The emphasis is on peace, truth and individual freedom of thought, with beliefs based on personal experiences and insights rather than blindly accepted declarations.

Among the countless controversies about Madame Blavatsky's life that continue to this day were her claims of a parade of manifested spirits during séances and an infamous photograph of her seated in front

of three "Ascended Masters" who material-
ized to pose with her: her master, El Myora;
an ermine-cloaked Saint Germain; and
her teacher, Kuthumi, through whom she
claimed to have channeled much of her
written work, including *The Secret Doctrine.*
Some researchers and associates at the
time took great delight in accusing her of
being a fraud, and there were those who
claimed that she admitted to her share of
hoaxes shortly before her death in 1891.

What Helena Blavatsky couldn't have
faked is the accuracy of many of the
prophecies she committed to paper, since
she didn't live long enough to see them
come to fruition.

Madame Blavatsky wrote *The Secret
Doctrine* in 1888, with or without the help of
her Ascended Master Kuthumi. In it she
said:

✳ "Between 1888 and 1897 there will be
a large rent made in the Veil of Nature,
and materialistic science will receive a
death-blow."

"Materialistic science" in this context referred to the way scientists of the time as-

sumed the world was only composed of its material, visible, tangible elements and approached it accordingly. That assumption changed forever when:

1895—Wilhelm Roentgen discovered X-rays, exposing a whole new universe of realities beyond the naked eye.

1896—Antoine Becquerel discovered radioactivity.

The Secret Doctrine also included descriptions of the reality of energy that had nothing to do with the beliefs of scientists in the 1800s. For example, Madame Blavatsky wrote in 1888 that:

✳ Atoms can be divided.
✳ Atoms are perpetually in motion.
✳ Matter and energy can be converted.

And then, sure enough, after her death in 1891:

1897—Sir J. J. Thomson discovered the electron.

1900—Max Planck's work laid the

foundation for the quantum theory of physics.

1905—Albert Einstein unveiled the theory of relativity, also known as $E=mc^2$, familiar even to those of us who don't know the first thing about physics.

Einstein's niece, incidentally, claimed that her famous, brilliant uncle kept a copy of Madame Blavatsky's *The Secret Doctrine* on his desk.

Helena Blavatsky's insights and prophecies weren't limited to science. She also had a thing or two to say about Atlantis—far too many to quote here, actually, but you'll get the idea:

* "That the periodical sinking and reappearance of mighty continents, now called Atlantean [Atlantis] and Lemurian [Lemuria] by modern writers, is no fiction will be demonstrated. It is only in the twentieth century that portions, if not the whole, of the present work will be vindicated."

* "The elevated ridge in the Atlantic basin, 9,000 feet in height, which runs

from a point near the British Islands, first slopes towards South America, then shifts almost at right angles to proceed in a south-easterly line toward the African coast . . . This ridge is a remnant of an Atlantic continent . . . Could it be traced further, it would establish the reality of a submarine horseshoe junction with a former continent in the Indian Ocean."

✳ "An impenetrable veil of secrecy was thrown over the occult and religious mysteries taught [there], after the submersion of the last remnant of the Atlantean race, some 12,000 years ago."

As luck, time, effort and a lot of genius would have it, that ridge Helena Blavatsky was describing really *could* be traced further, and was, by satellite photographs, some of which were shown and described in *Discover* magazine in March of 1996, more than a century after Madame Blavatsky committed her images to paper:

The Midatlantic Ridge snakes down the center of that ocean off Greenland to the latitude of Cape Horn . . . Under South Africa, the Southwest Indian Ridge shoots into the Indian Ocean like a fizzling rocket, or perhaps like the trail of some giant and cartoonish deep-sea mole.

Or, when you look at the satellite photos, like the second leg of a horseshoe.

A 1954 issue of *Geological Society of America,* reporting on the exploration of the summit of this Midatlantic Ridge, seems to confirm that Madame Blavatsky's mention of the submersion of the Atlantean race twelve thousand years ago might not be too far off:

The state of lithification of the limestone suggests that it may have been lithified under subaerial [i.e., above water, on land surface] conditions and that the sea mount [summit] may have been an island within the past 12,000 years.

And then there was this, also from 1888's *The Secret Doctrine:*

✳ "England is on the eve of such or another catastrophe; France, nearing such a point of her cycle, and Europe in general threatened with, or rather, on the eve of a cataclysm."

Twenty-six years later, the blink of an eye in the context of history, Germany would declare war on Russia and France, England would declare war on Germany, and the first of two world wars would begin, which would leave indelible scars on Great Britain, France and the rest of Europe and almost make the word "cataclysm" look like an understatement.

As I said earlier, Madame Helena Blavatsky lived a complex, controversial and, yes, undoubtedly imperfect life. I've only scratched its surface in these pages, and again, if you find yourselves inspired to dig more deeply, you'll be fascinated at the very least.

As for the ongoing debate about whether or not she was a legitimate psychic and medium, I'm frankly not very interested. In the end that boils down to "Yes, she was" versus "No, she wasn't," and I hope we've all got better things to do with our time than that.

Was she a prophet? I repeat, I've only given you glimpses of her prophecies, and you know I'm the first to encourage you to do your own research and come to your own informed conclusions. But I don't mind telling you, I'm impressed.

Lucia dos Santos and the Fatima Prophecies

I should clarify right from the beginning that Lucia dos Santos herself is *not* a prophet, but her story and the story of the Fatima Prophecies are too remarkable not to acknowledge, particularly out of respect for Sister Lucia and Pope John Paul II, both of whom are still alive at this writing. Lucia dos Santos exemplifies beautifully that prophecies aren't just given to the sophisticated. Sometimes they're presented to the innocent, the unsuspecting and the very young.

On May 13, 1917, three children named Jacinta, age seven, Francisco, age nine, and Lucia, age eleven, took their family's flock of sheep to graze in a hollow called the Cova da Iria, near the town of Fatima, Portugal. They were playing while the sheep grazed when suddenly they saw a brilliant flash of light. Confused and frightened by what appeared to be lightning from a cloudless sky, they had begun gathering the sheep and starting for home when a second flash of light appeared. They ran, even more frightened, until they stopped to stare at the sight of a Lady, dressed in white more radiant than the brightest sun, standing above a small tree.

"Don't be afraid," the Lady reassured them. "I come from Heaven, to ask that you come here for six months in succession, on the thirteenth day, at this same hour. I will tell you at that time who I am and what I want."

There were more messages and more instructions from the Lady, after which she seemed to disappear into a cloud of light.

The children told their parents about the experience, and Lucia's mother punished her for lying and then refusing to admit the lie. News of the children's story spread through the village, and they were subjected to relentless ridicule.

But when the thirteenth of each month came, the children went to the Cova da Iria, and the Lady never disappointed them. By the second month, curious crowds had begun following the children to the apparition site. The crowds continued to grow as the months went on, even though no one but the children could actually hear or see the Lady as she shared great secrets with them and promised a miracle in October that would make everyone believe.

On October 13, 1917, a crowd estimated at seventy thousand followed Lucia, Jacinta and Francisco to the Cova da Iria through a hard, relentless rain. The Lady appeared at the stroke of noon, and as she'd told them she would on their first meeting in May, she revealed to the children who she was and what she wanted.

"I am the Lady of the Rosary," she told them, "and I would like a chapel built on this site in my honor."

As the Blessed Mother ascended again, She opened Her hands toward the sky. All three children saw, in the sky, the Mysteries of the Rosary, followed by Joseph, Mary and the infant Jesus, who blessed the crowd. Then only Lucia saw the Virgin Mary beside Her resurrected Son.

In the meantime, the throngs were transfixed by the very different spectacle they were witnessing instead in that same place in the sky. The rain stopped and the sun appeared. Then, impossibly, the sun began dancing in the sky, whirling, erupting in a rainbow of fire that reflected a kaleidoscope of color on the faces of the crowd. Finally, with no warning, in one swift, awesome lunge, the sun appeared to be hurtling out of the sky toward the assembled masses, terrifying them, convincing many at that moment that the end of the world had come. But in a matter of seconds and just as quickly, it reversed its direction, returned to the sky and resumed its normal benign persona. Only after the seventy thousand had begun to recover from their panic and their wonder at what they'd seen did they notice that despite the steady rain they'd stood in for hours, their clothing and the ground around them were completely dry.

O Seculo, a newspaper in nearby Lisbon, sent its very skeptical editor, Avelino de Almeida, to report on what he was sure was a whole lot of needless hysteria over three children's overactive imaginations. But an excerpt from his article read:

> One could see the immense multitude turn toward the sun, which appeared free from clouds and in its zenith. It looked like a plaque of dull silver and it was possible to look at it without the least discomfort. It might have been an eclipse which was taking place. But at that moment a great shout went up and one could hear the spectators nearest at hand shouting: "A miracle! A miracle!" Before the astonished eyes of the crowd . . . the sun trembled, made sudden incredible movements outside any cosmic laws—the sun "danced."

As the Virgin Mary had asked, a shrine was built on the site of the visions. Jacinta and Francisco both tragically died in a terrible influenza plague within three years of that miraculous October day in 1917. Lucia entered a convent and continued to have occasional visits from the Blessed Mother, who, in 1927, gave Lucia permission to reveal two of the three prophecies that were given solely to the children during Her July

13 appearance. The third prophecy was not to be made public before 1960.

In the first prophecy of July 13, 1917, Mary told the children that the war—World War I—would end soon, as it did the following year. She then went on to say that "a night illuminated by an unknown light" would precede a "worse war." World War II began in 1939. On January 25, 1938, a stunning aurora borealis stretched across the northern sky with such brilliance that it was visible across Europe.

In the second prophecy, Our Lady of Fatima warned that Russia would "spread her errors throughout the world, promoting wars . . . Various nations will be annihilated. If people attend to My request for the consecration of Russia to My immaculate heart, Russia will be converted." In 1984 Pope John Paul II consecrated Russia, which many believe fulfilled the prophecy and led to the subsequent collapse, or conversion, of the Soviet Union.

As for the third prophecy, Lucia wrote it down, sealed it in an envelope with instructions that it wasn't to be opened and read until 1960, and gave it to a bishop in Portugal, who in turn presented it to the Vatican.

When 1960 came, Pope John XXIII reportedly unsealed the envelope but refused to reveal its contents, offering no more explanation than "This prophecy does not relate to my time." Pope John Paul II is said to have read it as well, a few days after he was elected in 1978.

The prophecy seems to refer to a "Bishop clothed in white," i.e., the Pope, who, as he makes his way with great effort through the throngs, falls to the ground, apparently dead, under a burst of gunfire.

On May 13, 1981, sixty-four years to the day after the Virgin's first appearance to the three children in the Cova da Iria, there was an assassination attempt on the life of Pope John Paul II by a Turkish gunman in St. Peter's Square. But it appeared to His Holiness that a "motherly hand . . . guided the bullet's path," allowing the "dying Pope" to halt "at the threshhold of death." He thanked the Mother Herself for saving his life. The potentially fatal bullet was given by the Pope to the bishop of Leiria-Fatima, who had it set in the crown of the statue of Our Lady Of Fatima at the shrine in Her honor.

On May 13, 2000, Pope John Paul II visited Sister Lucia dos Santos, who by now was ninety-three years old and a Carmelite nun. He also beatified Jacinta and Francisco Marto, the other two witnesses to the apparitions, who are buried near the Virgin's shrine. Never before or since has the Roman Catholic Church beatified children who weren't martyrs.

On May 14, 2000, to a crowd of 600,000, the Vatican announced the long-awaited contents of the third prophecy of Fatima, the foretelling of the assassination attempt on the Pope.

But some wonder why, if that's all the information contained in the third prophecy, the Vatican waited so long to reveal its contents. Or why in 1996 Cardinal Joseph Ratzinger, representing the Vatican, announced during a radio broadcast that there was "nothing worrisome" in the prophecy and that the Vatican was only keeping its contents secret to avoid "confusing religious prophecy with sensationalism." Many find that to be a very odd description of a message limited to the vision of what by then was the long-passed, unsuccessful attempt to take the life of Pope John Paul II. And so there are those who say the mystery of the third prophecy has yet to be solved.

Pilgrimages to the shrine of the Blessed Virgin continue to this day, in reverent homage to Our Lady of Fatima but also in respect for three young children who, for reasons only God needs to know, were entrusted with prophecies from the mouth of the Holy Mother Herself.

H. G. Wells

H. G. Wells was a novelist, of course, as well as a journalist and a historian, and his stature as a prophet may get blurred a little by his equal stature as a science fiction writer with such a passionate curiosity about the future that he became known in literary circles and beyond as "the Man Who Invented Tomorrow."

He was born in England in 1866 to working-class parents and was as innately drawn to books as other children his age were to sports and toys. His mother occasionally worked as a housekeeper at a nearby estate, and he would go with her for the sole purpose of sneaking into the library and spending as many hours there reading as her job would allow.

His school years were interrupted through no fault of his own by work as a draper's apprentice, which he hated. He finally returned to school with an emphasis on the sciences in general and biology in particular, but left without graduating. He taught in private schools and didn't complete his B.S. degree until three years later. Three years after that, in 1893, after teaching again, this time at a correspondence college, he became a full-time writer.

But please don't get the impression that he wasn't devoting any attention to his personal life through all this, and apparently being just as flawed and shortsighted about it as the rest of us. In 1891, the year after he received his degree, he married his cousin Isabel. During that marriage he worked two jobs to support both her and his parents and ended up with tuberculosis. He then left Isabel for one of his students, a young woman named Amy Catherine Robbins, and married her in 1895. If you think you're detecting the beginnings of a lifelong pattern, you're right.

H. G. Wells's first novel was an expression of his most obsessive passion. It was called *The Time Machine,* and it involved a man who'd just returned from a trip to the future, or more precisely the year 802701. On some levels *The Time Machine* is a parody, and on many levels it's pure dark science fiction. But the technical details and the basic principles of the machine expressed a depth in the book, and in Wells, that the literary world wasn't expecting. Einstein was still years away from publishing his theory of the time-space continuum that *The Time Machine* alluded to, and H. G. Wells began attracting attention not only as a writer but also as a man who might have some insights into the future that weren't really fiction at all.

He continued with several more science fiction groundbreakers, including *The War of the Worlds* and *The Island of Dr. Moreau,* and his success grew, along with his conflicted, outspoken and sometimes radical ideas about social consciousness. He was a champion of the lower classes, for example, and was such a passionate believer in a fairer society that he joined a London socialist organization called the Fabian Society. But he and its leaders, particularly

George Bernard Shaw, constantly quarreled, and he used the Society as the basis for his novel *The New Machiavelli*. He believed strongly in sexual freedom, which he displayed by infidelity to his wife that was almost constant until her death in 1927, and he was a strong advocate of birth control, which makes his two legitimate children by Amy and his five illegitimate children by various mistresses seem like a serious conflict in retrospect.

The sincerity of his belief that, bleak as the future might be because of man's inhumanity to man, it was still worth fighting for, catapulted him into a prolific array of nonfiction work, including *The Outline of History,* which was the twentieth century's second best seller at the time and gained him celebrity status. He became a member of the Research Committee for the League of Nations, had meetings with Lenin, Stalin and Roosevelt and was even a candidate for the British Parliament. It's sometimes overlooked that of the one hundred plus books that H. G. Wells wrote in his lifetime, only about half of them were novels.

The story goes that Wells had gone off by himself one night at a party. One of the other guests noticed and asked what he was doing.

"I'm writing my epitaph," he said.

"What will it say?" The guest half-smiled, convinced that Wells was kidding.

He looked at her with unamused resignation and replied, "It will simply read, 'God damn you all, I told you so.' "

H. G. Wells died on August 13, 1946.

His traceable prophecies include:

* the atomic bomb
* England's entering a world war in 1940
* the London Blitz
* the military vehicle we know as the tank
* the military use of airplanes
* superhighways
* computers
* overcrowded cities
* bombs made of uranium
* VCRs
* television sets, which would broadcast the news

Perhaps the prophecy of H. G. Wells's that first drew me to him and made me read further was that if—and only if—humanity would change enough to avoid destroying itself, he envisioned a world of peace, free from old hatreds, bigotry and class-consciousness, by the middle of the twenty-first century. I don't care how depressed, conflicted and self-indulgent the messenger might have been who passed that along. Who among us doesn't experience all of those emotions in our lives, in one degree or another? I'll happily and proudly help broadcast any reminder that we have no business sitting back and complaining about our fear of the dark without lifting a finger to turn on the Light.

Edgar Cayce

Edgar Cayce is one of the prophets I've admired most and found most compelling in my decades of study. To those who dismiss him as a fraud, I'd just like to say, "He helped countless people during his lifetime. How many have you helped?"

Not only did Edgar Cayce come upon his clairvoyant and prophetic gifts completely by accident, but he also never had any conscious access to them. He was known as "the Sleeping Prophet" with good reason—he performed all his readings, healings, spiritual and metaphysical dictations and prophecies while he was in a deep state of self-induced, trance-like, hypnotic sleep, none of which he had any memory of when he was awake.

Edgar Cayce was born in 1877, on a farm in Kentucky. He was neither a good student nor a good reader, and his formal education ended with grammar school. He was earning a modest living as a photographer when, in his early twenties, an illness caused him to lose his voice. A year of various medical treatments didn't restore it to anything more than a hoarse whisper, and he finally took a friend's advice to try hypnotism, since all else had failed.

His friend accompanied him to a local hypnotist, where Cayce suggested it would be easiest if he put himself to sleep, which he'd always been able to do. Once he was "under," in a deep trance, Cayce's friend and the hypnotist witnessed an amazing phenomenon: Edgar Cayce, who, between his grammar school education and his disinterest in reading, had a knowledge of the human anatomy amounting to zero, gave a precise description and diagnosis of exactly what had caused the condition in his throat, as if he were a skilled physician studying an X-ray. He then gave the hypnotist a list of physiological suggestions/instructions to repeat back to him over and over again while he was still in his trance, suggestions about blood flowing and vocal cords relaxing and arteries opening to restore oxygen and life to specific paralyzed muscles. The hypnotist did as he was told, Cayce followed his own instructions as repeated to him by the hypnotist, and he awoke from that session with his full voice restored for the first time in a year.

Between his friend, his family and the hypnotist, word spread very quickly about this amazing man who seemed to have the power to both diagnose and recommend cures for illnesses in his "sleep." He was immediately flooded with requests from people begging him to do the same for them or a sick loved one, and his first reaction was to decline—not because he didn't want to help, but because no one was more aware than he was how completely uneducated he was and how inadequate he felt offering the kind of help he was being asked for. And it's worth repeating, he had no waking memory of what had happened during his hypnosis session, and no clue how he'd managed to accomplish what he was being asked to do again by all these strangers, who seemed to think he could make them well when so many experienced doctors had failed.

The one thing he couldn't argue with, though, was that, whether he knew how it had happened or not, he'd cured himself somehow, and thanks to some follow-up hypnosis sessions, the cure became an obviously permanent one. If he really did have a gift that would allow him to offer diagnoses and remedies to people, how could he live with himself if he refused to at least try?

Edgar Cayce rarely met his "clients." Instead, they came to him in the form of letters, often mailed from hundreds of miles away. Cayce would lie down on the couch and loosen his necktie and shoelaces. His wife Gertrude would give him the only information he required for each reading: the subject's full name, address and exactly where he or she would be at the agreed upon time of the reading. Gertrude would then ask her husband relevant questions during the reading, while his secretary, Gladys Davis, sat nearby, steno pad in hand, recording the reading in shorthand. After Cayce had put himself "under," he would eventually signal the start of the reading with the words "Yes, we have the body."

Cayce continued these "physical" readings throughout his life. But they turned out to be only the beginning, thanks to a man named Arthur Lammers, a printer Cayce happened to meet in the course of his photography business in 1923. Lammers was fascinated by the world of metaphysics— questions about the meaning of life, the nature of the human soul, death and the afterlife, and so on—and asked Edgar Cayce for a kind of reading he'd never done before, a reading in which, while he was "under" as usual, he would allow Lammers to ask those kinds of questions to see what answers Cayce's "sleeping" mind would come up with.

That was the first of more than two thousand sessions that came to be known as "life readings," in which Cayce offered information about "clients' " past lives and expanded that information into a whole world of metaphysical philosophy that was completely foreign to his strict Protestant upbringing. It took him some time to make peace with the differences between what he thought he'd always "known," and even taught for years in Sunday school, and what his "sleeping" mind seemed to "know" with far greater certainty.

But ultimately Edgar Cayce's readings led him to what he felt was, for him, an inescapable belief in reincarnation, and in the fact that in their heart of hearts and soul of souls, all the great religions of the world share the same basic principles.

An essential part of Cayce's greatness is that he never took an ounce of credit for any of the information that came through him and out of his mouth. Instead, he explained (while "under," of course) that he was simply accessing information from the subconscious minds of his subjects, and from the Akashic Records, which are the collective, infinite memories and histories, kept on the Other Side, of every thought, moment, word and event in the circle we call eternity.

Edgar Cayce lived very modestly throughout his life and refused to get rich from his gifts. He worked much too hard for much too long, until finally he suffered a stroke from which he never recovered. He died on January 3, 1945, leaving behind a body of work that included more than fourteen thousand readings, the transcripts of which have inspired more than three hundred books about his work. His readings included medical issues, of course, and reincarnation, and metaphysical philosophies, and meditation and dreams.

And they most certainly included prophecies:

* He predicted the beginning and end of both World War I and World War II.
* He predicted, in 1939, the death of two sitting presidents. (Franklin Roosevelt died in 1945, and John Kennedy was assassinated in 1963, both of them while in office.)
* In 1935 he predicted the approaching cataclysm in Europe involving Germany, Austria and eventually Japan.
* He also predicted a potential third world war "in Libya, and in Egypt, in

Ankara, and in Syria; through the straits around those areas above Australia, in the Indian Ocean and the Persian Gulf."

He believed strongly in the ancient existence of a highly advanced civilization on the lost continent of Atlantis, and that someday Atlantis would reemerge from beneath the ocean.

There are prophecies of Edgar Cayce's that haven't come true. I wouldn't presume to speak for him, but my guess would be that his explanation for that would be similar to mine when I find out I was wrong about a reading or a prediction. Any prophet, psychic, clairvoyant, medium or other paranormalist who claims to be accurate 100 percent of the time is a fraud and a liar. Only God is right 100 percent of the time. All the rest of us can do is receive and transmit information we're given, and stay out of the way as best we can. We can't take credit for any of the information, but blame for inaccuracy falls justifiably on our shoulders, because it means that somewhere along the line we misspoke, misunderstood, misinterpreted and/or somehow involuntarily interfered, and the messages suffered in the translation.

But no one tried harder, or with more humility, or with more of an open, unjudging mind, or with more selflessness and commitment, at the expense of his own physical and financial well-being, to get it right for the right reasons than the almost reluctantly gifted Sleeping Prophet, Edgar Cayce.

I'm afraid I've only scratched the surface of the prophets I've studied and been fascinated by over all these years. There are many others, from such famous ones as Eileen Garrett, Maria Esperanza, Mother Shipton and Aldous Huxley, to the unexpected and understated prophetic visions of Abraham Lincoln's. Each of them warrants every moment of exploration you care to give them. Believe them or disbelieve them, embrace them or dismiss them, just approach them with an open mind and an absolute determination to draw your own conclusions about their validity and about the gift of prophecy in general—not my conclusions, or your family's, or your friends', or your church's, or whatever you perceive society's to be, but *yours,* based on facts, information and the common sense that tells you where "lucky guesses" leave off and genuine prophecy begins.

A Word About False Prophets

A repairman came to the house one day last fall. Perfectly sweet, perfectly polite. After he'd been here awhile, I happened to stroll into the kitchen where he was working and found him holding and staring at the cover for this book. Dutton had just sent an early copy of the cover, which I'd apparently set aside on the counter nearby.

He looked a little embarrassed that I'd caught him. Then he noticed my picture on the cover, did a double take and asked, "Is this you?"

"Yes, it is," I said.

"You wrote a prophecy book?" he asked.

"Yes, I did," I told him.

He set the book cover down, still seeming a bit awkward. Trying to put him at ease, I added, "You know, if you'll give me your name and address before you leave, I'll be happy to send you a copy of the book when it comes out."

"No, thank you," he said, turning back to my broken dishwasher. "I don't read that kind of thing. I'm a Christian."

I'm sixty-eight. I've been doing this all my life. I'm pretty accustomed to the fact that people seem to feel free to say almost anything to me. One of my favorites is "Wow, you're really very attractive in person. I'm surprised. You're so ugly on TV." Not to mention every adjective—and I mean *every* adjective—synonymous with crazy, insane, loony and nuts. And you know what? Almost without exception, it doesn't bother me. Find me attractive, or don't. Believe I'm psychic, believe there are such things as psychics at all, or don't. But never, never doubt that anything I've ever done, or anything I ever will do, isn't devoted to, driven by, because of, made possible by and in the heartfelt service of our Lord and of God Himself.

It's not that the repairman caught me completely off guard. This isn't the first or the hundredth time I've run into that attitude, and as a passionate student of the Bible, I'm well aware that it clearly states, in Matthew 7:15, "Beware of false prophets, which come to you in sheep's clothing, but inwardly they are ravening wolves." And, in Leviticus 19:31, "Do not turn to mediums or wizards; do not seek them out to be defiled by them." And in Jeremiah 27:9, "Harken not to your prophets, nor to your diviners, nor to your dreamers."

So how can I, a Gnostic Christian—adoring every celebration of our connection to our Creator no matter what name He's called by on this earth, worshiping God with every breath I take—openly embrace the prophets I've discussed in this chapter, or have the nerve to offer prophecies of my own? How do you know that all of them and I are not those same false prophets Jesus warned against?

The easy answer, of course, is to say that any prophet who tries to lead you farther away from God is a false prophet. But any false prophet who's even slightly effective is bound to be a good manipulator, and the first thing a good manipulator does is put on a great show of expertise at whatever subject is nearest and dearest to the hearts of those he or she is trying to manipulate. If that subject happens to be God, then the false prophet is bound to claim that knowledge and love of God far more than you've ever dreamed of and that by becoming closer to the prophet you'll actually come closer to Him. Very seductive, and a guaranteed lie.

I do want to put to rest the idea that prophets and prophecies are "the work of the devil." The very same Bible that warns us against false prophets makes that very clear—not to mention the fact that I don't happen to believe in an actual being called "the devil" or Satan to begin with. No, I believe with all my heart that evil is an invention of those spirits who turn away from God—who *never* turns away from us. And if there were a devil, he would never have a shadow of the power of our Creator, to whom we owe thanks for every one of our blessings, including the gifts we're given. It's God and no one else who gives humankind our gifts. It's how we use those gifts that determines whether they're "good" or "evil." And chances are, the only gifts false prophets have been given are the gifts of mind control and thinly disguised narcissism.

When you listen closely to false prophets, you'll realize that they're not interested in your worshiping God as much as they're interested in your worshiping them, as if they're the only available direct line between you and God. They direct all prayers, all Scripture readings and most certainly all scripture interpretations. Forget what you've always believed or been taught to believe were God's laws and commandments. The false prophets will tell you that they and only they know the truth of what God intended and what He has in store, which is why they're worthy of your slavish obedience. According to their convenient prophecies, which they claim just happen to come from God, following even their most insane orders is your only hope of salvation.

To make sure that no one can possibly talk any sense into you or point out their inevitable contradictions, false prophets will almost always begin isolating you from your family, friends, coworkers and everyone else who knows and cares about you. Often with carefully selected out-of-context Scripture quotations, they will portray anyone who criticizes them or questions their motives as being evil. It's a classic case of the pot calling the kettle black and a truly Godless act to make you choose between one person and all these other people who've always loved you and wanted the best for you. But the only way a false prophet can take hold is in a vacuum where no other information but the prophet's is allowed inside.

Many false prophets will also find countless ways to separate you from your money at every possible opportunity. On the grandest scale, they'll demand that their followers take a vow of poverty and give up all their worldly possessions, invariably to the "prophets" themselves, since, let's face it, God has no use for money. The psychology is simple: not only are most false prophets in it for the money, the power or both, but they also know that the less their followers have, the needier, more dependent and less self-confident they'll be.

False prophets tend to make up their own rules for their behavior at their own narcissistic whim, having nothing to do with God's rules whatsoever, but then cite a message from God as their excuse when the need arises, as if God bends his own rules sometimes for their personal convenience. False prophets have used the message-from-God excuse for everything from adultery to murder to mass suicide, telling us nothing about God and everything about how low false prophets will really stoop in their obsessive need for power and determination to extinguish the true Light of the loving, uniting, pacifistic God who created us.

You'll never hear a false prophet admit to the possibility of being wrong. Their prophecies will either tend to be so vague that they could apply to almost anything, or they will claim that any that appear to be inaccurate are the fault of the interpreter. And anyone who accuses them of doing something wrong or, God forbid, illegal, is tragically, unfairly persecuting them, giving them the opportunity to be both felons and martyrs.

In summary, then, I couldn't agree more with Matthew 7:15. "Beware of false prophets" by all means! Just be clear on who they are, who they most certainly are not, and what they're after, so you won't find yourself turning away from those who might have something of value to say.

✳ Any prophet who feels your attention and adoration should be divided equally between God and the prophet is a false prophet.

✳ Any prophet who claims to have a closer relationship with God than you do, or to be more special in His eyes than you are, is a false prophet.

✳ Any prophet who claims you need him or her in order to communicate with God is a false prophet.

✳ Any prophet who insists that you embrace the prophet's thoughts and opinions rather than exploring and forming your own is a false prophet.

✳ Any prophet whose power depends on isolating you from those who've loved, supported and been honest with you is a false prophet.

✳ Any prophet who asks you to jeopardize or sacrifice your stability or your financial security, especially in the form of a "donation" to the prophet or his or her "church," or whatever the organization is called, is a false prophet.

✳ Any prophet who tells you that only he or she knows the truth of what God has in store for you, for your future or for humankind is a false prophet.

✳ Any prophet who believes that anyone who criticizes or disagrees with him or her is evil or deserving of retribution is a false prophet.

✳ Any prophet whose ultimate goal is accumulating adoring followers more for the prophet than for God is a false prophet.

✳ Any prophet who believes he or she is exempt from the laws of God and society and somehow in a position of divine immunity from consequence is a false prophet.

✳ Any prophet who claims to be infallible is a false prophet.

✳ Any prophet who financially gains from his or her gift without seeing to it that worthy causes and the less fortunate are enriched as well by those financial gains is a false prophet. Selfishness, ingratitude and any other form of arrogance, financial or otherwise, toward the very people a psychic, medium, clairvoyant or prophet is here to serve is a guarantee that either the God-given gift will vanish or that there was never a God-given gift to begin with.

To really understand the sincere, genuinely gifted prophet, it makes all the difference in the world to really understand where the prophetic information comes from. The more mysterious, mystical and exclusive a prophet's source of information seems, the more mysterious, mystical and exclusive the prophet is likely to seem. The far more interesting truth is that genuine prophets are simply tapping into an infinite wealth of facts to which every one of us has had access since eternity began and will have access to again when we're back Home on the Other Side.

CHAPTER THREE

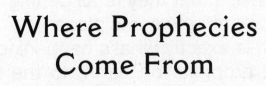

Where Prophecies Come From

So how do a sixteenth-century French physician, a Russian medium, a British prime minister, two English authors and a farmer's son from Kentucky all come up with such uncannily similar prophecies about world wars, atom bombs and lost continents? Skeptics might try to put up an argument for coincidence. And why not? It's so easy for them to just sweep everything they don't understand under a nice big "coincidence" rug, and who cares if the odds against the coincidence are too astronomical to calculate? But those of us who prefer a less lazy, more logical answer find it hard to resist an obvious conclusion: when such diverse people from different centuries and different parts of the world seem to have the same information, maybe it just makes sense that they're all getting that information from the same place.

Which is exactly what's happening. From the first prophets on earth, to the Biblical prophets and the American Indians and the Aborigines and the Hindus and Buddha, to the past and present prophets of modern civilization, to all the prophets still to come, prophecies originate from one common source, eternal, infinite and infallible: our birthplace and our destination, a place as real as we are called the Other Side.

My book *Life on The Other Side* describes in detail the fact that when our spirits leave our bodies in this transition called "death," we don't just go floating around on clouds for the rest of eternity playing harps and waving at passing Angels. Instead, our brief trips to earth, which can best be described as "boot camp," are simply interruptions, of our own choosing, in our very full, very busy lives back Home, which we return to when we've finished what we came here to accomplish.

Once we understand a few of the specifics of the Other Side, and of our lives there, we can understand far more easily how prophecies occur and what the gift of prophecy is all about. I'm actually tempted to replace the word "understand" with the word "remember" in that sentence, since you already know everything I'm about to tell you as well as I do. Your spirit mind, the eternal part of you that always was and always will be, has perfect retention of every moment you've lived, both on the Other Side and in all your incarnations on earth. Those memories are stored in the depths of the subconscious, where they can be accessed during deep hypnosis or meditation or, as in Edgar Cayce's experience, sleep. But even the conscious mind gets occasional glimpses of them—when you meet a total stranger, for example, whom you feel you've known all your life, or visit a place you've never been before and can find your way around as if you grew up there.

With apologies for openly plagiarizing myself, I'll give you in its entirety the same warning about this chapter that I gave the readers of *Life on The Other Side*: if and when a few descriptions strike an oddly familiar chord or two, don't let it startle you, and please don't think it's your imagination. Once upon a time, after all, you took your first breath, and your first baby step, and opened your eyes for the first time. The fact that you have no conscious memory of those moments doesn't mean they didn't happen. So while your conscious mind takes in these pages, pay attention to any quiet signals you might get from the spirit mind in your subconscious as it reads along. They aren't likely to be anything dramatic, just fleeting pangs of Homesickness.

The Other Side: A Few Basic Facts

As a licensed master hypnotist, I've taken literally thousands of people through past-life regressions, including reliving their deaths in those past lives. No matter what their culture or religion or race or upbringing, or beliefs or lack of them, they've described exactly what my decades of study indicated and my own near-death experience took me through. Sure enough, it wasn't wishful thinking after all, there really was a tunnel, with a brilliant white light at its end, the glowing embodiment of all the

love, wisdom, compassion, peace and joy
that is God. Not for an instant was there a
feeling of having died. Instead there was
just a great sensation of freedom, and of
something happening that was natural and
familiar and thrilling. Just as all roads once
led to Rome, all tunnels, no matter where
on this earth they begin, lead to the divine
glory of the Other Side.

The one surprise, that we all seem to forget from one incarnation to the next, is that
this tunnel we've all heard so much about
rises from our own bodies, from our own
etheric substance, and instead of pointing
upward into the sky, where we somehow always imagine heaven is, it stops in a position just above us, at a thirty- or forty-de-
gree angle, so that our trip through the
tunnel isn't really "up" at all, but "across."
And that's because, believe it or not, the
Other Side isn't "out there somewhere," it's
right here among us, a mere three feet
above our own ground level. It's another dimension, operating at a much higher vibra-
tional frequency than ours here on earth,
and duplicating the earth's topography almost identically.

When we arrive on the Other Side, what

we have to look forward to first is a reunion that can only be described as impossibly joyful. This isn't just the gathering we usually think of, in which the loved ones who predeceased us on earth are waiting to greet us. We're also surrounded by loved ones from past incarnations and from our lives on the Other Side, not to mention (my favorite part) every pet we've ever had in every life we've lived on earth. In fact, my Spirit Guide Francine tells me the people assembled for this ecstatic reunion have to wait their turn until all our beloved animals are finished welcoming us Home.

No matter where on this earth we die, the tunnel takes us to the same magnificent entrance on the Other Side, visible beyond the meadow where these reunions take place. This entrance is actually a hub of magnificent buildings—yes, there are buildings throughout the infinite landscape of the Other Side—each of which has its own specific purpose.

First and closest to us is the Hall of Wisdom, domed, pillared and Romanesque. Vast marble steps lead to its entrance, with graceful fountains, statuary and flowering vines softening the endless gleaming stone. The Hall of Wisdom, among other things, houses the Scanning Machine, where we literally view the earthly lives we've just lived, from the perspective of Home, with total recall of what it was we intended to accomplish when we chose to incarnate in the first place.

To the right of the Hall of Wisdom is the Hall of Justice, with its breathtaking Gardens. When you hear people who've had near-death experiences talk about fleeting memories of brilliant colors and fragrances and flowers and clear sparkling waterfalls beyond anything earth has to offer, for as far as the eye could see, as if nature itself had gathered in this one place to sing God its finest hymn of praise, it's a safe bet that before reentering their bodies, their spirits visited the Gardens of the Hall of Justice on the Other Side.

The Hall of Wisdom and the Hall of Justice sit in the shadow of the Towers, which are two identical contemporary monoliths of white marble and blue glass. Water gently streams down the walls of the buildings, misting the lush jasmine that seems to scent the Towers themselves for miles

around. The Towers are useful for new arrivals who need extra help with their transition back Home again, and they're
also cherished by the "locals" as gorgeous
places to study and meditate.

And last but certainly not least, completing the buildings that form the entrance to
the Other Side, we find the Hall of Records.

The Hall of Records

The Hall of Records sits to the immediate
left of the Hall of Wisdom. Its architecture is
classic Greco-Roman, and its most stunning feature is a towering dome that glitters
with magnificent authority above the surrounding hills.

While it's difficult to compare earthly
space to space on the Other Side, it's still
accurate to say that the Hall of Records is
vast by necessity. Just one of its functions
is to keep on file, in writing, every detailed
chart of every incarnation of every one of
the lifetimes each one of us has spent on
earth. (We'll deal with a brief discussion of
life charts momentarily, but they're exhaustively covered in *Life on The Other Side* and

many of my other books if you find you're still curious.) The Hall also contains the originals of every historical work ever written, including those whose earthly copies have been destroyed, from the libraries of Alexandria to all the brilliant literature that was lost with the continents of Atlantis and Lemuria.

And also preserved and appropriately worshiped in the Hall of Records are the actual Akashic Records.

You might remember their being mentioned in Chapter 2, as one of Edgar Cayce's answers to where his prophetic information came from.

He was right.

Most prophets, whether they realize it or not, receive a great deal of their information by spiritually, psychically or astrally tapping into the Akashic Records, deep in the endless, sacred aisles of a domed building in another dimension just three feet above us.

The Akashic Records

The Akashic Records have been described in a number of ways by a number of different people and cultures. Edgar Cayce knew them as the collective memories and histories of every thought, sound, vibration, moment and event in eternity. The Hindus thought of them as every thought, word and action, recorded on a substance called "akasha," which they believed was the primary principle of nature from which earth, water, fire and air were created. Psychologist Carl Jung called them the Collective Unconscious, a powerful conceptual force but not necessarily a literally recorded one.

The definition I prefer, use and strongly believe is that the Akashic Records are the written memory of God. I don't doubt for a moment that their impact is imprinted on the ether of the universe, the very atmosphere in which we exist, but I also know beyond all doubt that those records exist, in the universal language of Aramaic, on vast shelves in vast aisles, in the perfect air of the perfect rooms of the perfect sanctity of the Hall of Records, accessible to every one of us at any time, and most certainly accessible to every prophet since time began.

Life Charts

Before each of us comes to earth for another incarnation, we write an unbelievably detailed chart on the Other Side, mapping out the specifics of the lifetime we're about to live. We chart our mothers, our fathers, our children, our friends, our enemies, our spouses, our careers, our triumphs, our failures, our joys, our heartaches—I usually never get past the "mothers" thing without wondering if I might have been drunk when I wrote my chart, and chose the mother I ended up with and that's why I've always hated the taste of alcohol here on earth.

Our charts, which we really do literally write, on scrolls, are also housed in the Hall of Records. I'd love for you to take a moment to picture (or remember, since it's a sight your spirit mind knows and loves) how breathtaking it is to see endless aisle after endless aisle after endless aisle beneath that impossibly beautiful dome, each aisle filled with shelves for as far as the eye can see, each shelf filled with more scrolls than we can begin to count, each scroll in perfect order and perfect condition, on which is written every chart of every life ever lived by every spirit ever created by God since the beginning of time.

While we're here on earth, it's frustrating but true that we don't have access to our own charts. You may have heard me say that I'm not psychic about myself, nor have I met any psychic who's psychic about him or herself, and that's why. You and I are all likely to have a million intuitions in the course of our lives, and other signals that we *remember* our charts, but cheating and "reading ahead" is off limits until we get Home again.

What we can do while we're here on earth, though, is study other people's charts—someone in history, someone who's on earth at the same time we are or even someone who's still to come. We're not allowed to look at our own charts until we're on the Other Side again. It would be considered kind of the spiritual version of using "crib notes" during a test. We have three extraordinary ways in which we can study those charts:

* We can watch someone's chart unfold, just as we'll watch our own most

recent incarnation unfold when we return to the Other Side, at the Scanning Machine in the sacred Hall of Wisdom. The Scanning Machine is a huge convex dome of blue glass, inside of which all the events of the life we've just completed, or the life written in the chart we're studying, play out before our eyes in the form of a three-dimensional hologram, so that no matter where we move around the dome, we won't miss a single detail. (By the way, when people have had a near-death experience and refer to the sensation of their whole life flashing before their eyes, it's not just a sensation. It means they made it as far as the Scanning Machine before their spirit decided to return to their body and go on with life on earth for a while.)

* We can listen to a chart, in what amounts to kind of an ultra-auditory form of the Scanning Machine, books-on-tape meets virtual reality, multiplied by thousands.

* Or, we can actually "merge" with the chart, which essentially amounts to

climbing into the chart and living it
in total empathy, assimilating the
senses, feelings and reality of the person whose chart we're studying without ever losing our own identity.

Purely hypothetically, studying life charts
would allow Madame Blavatsky, let's say, to
stand at the Scanning Machine and actually
witness Einstein's discovery of the theory of
relativity. Or, for that matter, allow Winston
Churchill to "merge" with Franklin Roosevelt's chart and, through it, witness the
horror that Adolf Hitler had in store for the
world. (See *The Other Side and Back* or *Life
on The Other Side* if you're curious to know
why Churchill couldn't have simply read
Hitler's chart.)

Study and Research on the Other Side

As I said, when we leave our bodies on
earth and arrive on the Other Side, we're
anything but newcomers. God promised us
eternity, after all, and eternity doesn't just
mean "always will be," it also means "always were." So our arrival on the Other

Side is a Homecoming, a return to established lives and relationships and work and
study that bring us joy.

Yes, it's true, on the Other Side, work and
study are a joy, as is everything we do
there. It wouldn't be paradise if that weren't
true, let's face it. The moment we reclaim
our lives back Home, we also reclaim the
full potential of our minds, as well as the cu-
mulative memories, wisdom, intellect and
insight of our eternal past. And even with an
eternity to live, and the facile God-given
minds we're blessed with on the Other
Side, the exciting truth is that not one of us
will ever know everything there is to know
and learn everything there is to learn.
There's only one all-knowing Being in this
universe, and He created the rest of us. Fortunately, He also created a universe so infinitely complex that it's impossible for us to
run out of subjects to explore. And at
Home, there's no course of study that's not
available, taught by the most enlightened
minds ever conceived.

As much as we value our studies on the
Other Side for ourselves, we also devote
tireless, passionate effort to research on behalf of others, in every area from medicine

to science to psychology to sociology to ecology. It's certainly not for the benefit of our fellow residents at Home, since there's no disease there, no drought, no pollution, no hunger, no mental illness, no problems or unhappiness or discomfort of any kind, just perfect bliss in the constant immediate presence of God, the Messiah and the Angels.

Instead, it's for the benefit of the planets to which the spirits on the Other Side choose to incarnate from time to time. (And could we please get over this ludicrous notion that in a universe so infinite we haven't even begun to fathom its size yet, our tiny earth is the only populated planet?) There's no question that we eternally cherish the Other Side as Home, first, foremost and above all. But we reserve a special place in our hearts for earth, and the other planets we occupy, as our homes away from Home. We fondly watch over those flawed, struggling worlds where we've learned and tried and failed and won and lost and loved and grieved and left and returned to do it better. We know those worlds, we understand them; history and compassion tie us to them and we want to help.

Fortunately, on the Other Side, we have the resources, the expertise and the determination to accomplish anything and everything we set our minds to, and there are schools, libraries, research centers and laboratories everywhere, constantly bustling with activity and celebration. We study and research and invent and strive to cure on the Other Side because it is our debt and our privilege to contribute to a universe we embrace as a community and the God who made it ours to watch over. At every moment the search at Home continues for cures for cancer, AIDS, Parkinson's disease, Alzheimer's disease, multiple sclerosis and every other illness that threatens human health. Cleaner fuel sources are explored, as well as agricultural advancements to solve the earthly hunger crisis, permanent physiological solutions for substance addictions and countless mental imbalances, space transports that will make interplanetary travel as commonplace as travel from one side of the globe to the other—there's literally no limit to the subject matter, the progress and the success rate of the spirit minds on the Other Side, unencumbered as they are by such earthly road-

blocks as greed, politics and stupefying bureaucracy.

Infused Knowledge

You may already be familiar with the term
"infused knowledge." But in case it's new to
you, it's a direct transfer of information from
one mind to another with no conscious
awareness on the part of the receiver of
where that information came from. For example, you go to sleep one night with a
problem weighing on your mind, and you
wake up the next morning knowing exactly
how to solve it. I'm not talking about a solution that comes as a result of your mind finally being relaxed enough during sleep to
think clearly. That's not infused knowledge,
that's just the common bonus of a good
night's sleep. I'm talking about a solution
that comes from a new bit of information, a
piece of the puzzle you weren't aware of
before, something you might even convince
yourself you remembered while you slept,
but the more you think about it, the more
you realize you can't have "remembered"
something that was news to you.

Infused knowledge is one of the most common ways that the spirit world on the Other Side communicates with our spirits, wide-awake and thriving in our subconscious minds, here on earth. Our subconscious minds are obviously most accessible when our cluttered conscious minds are as far out of the way as possible—while we sleep, under hypnosis, during meditation or sometimes when we're simply very tired. And then there are those whose subconscious minds are just naturally more readily and frequently available to infused knowledge from the Other Side, whether they're aware of it or not.

It's through those minds that the Other Side shares the results of all its study and research, so that cures, breakthroughs, inventions and other great contributions to humankind can manifest themselves on earth. I'm sure you've noticed that very often brilliant minds on opposite sides of the globe seem to come up with virtually identical discoveries almost simultaneously. Now you know why. It's because spirits on the Other Side, through infused knowledge, have successfully delivered information to those in this world who have the wisdom, dedication, experience, open-mindedness, expertise and talent to act on that information and make it a useful, worthwhile reality. This collaboration between the earth and Home is really the ultimate interdependent partnership. Researchers on the Other Side need their colleagues on earth to put practical form and function to the results of their research, and those colleagues need some divine intervention from the Other Side to help overcome this earth's enormous obstacles. And without the silent blessing of infused knowledge, that God-made collaboration could never take place.

It's no big surprise, then, that infused knowledge from Home is also one of the ways in which prophets receive information. A physicist in a laboratory on the Other Side transmitting the information to a physicist on earth that atoms can be divided is one thing. Transmitting it to someone who doesn't know one end of a microscope from the other doesn't suddenly obligate the receiver to understand how to divide an atom, or why anyone would want to, or even necessarily what an atom is to begin with. The obligation of prophets who receive infused knowledge beyond their scope, control or power isn't to editorialize or try to make sense of it, it's simply to repeat it as accurately as possible to whoever might find it useful. Edgar Cayce's letter readings are a perfect example of a prophet's compassionate, responsible handling of infused knowledge. With no medical or anatomical education whatsoever, Cayce, in a self-induced trance to access his spirit mind, offered diagnoses and cures that proved over and over and over again to be effective and even life-saving for the thousands who wrote him. No interference with the information on Cayce's part, no self-aggrandizing, no waking assumption that by some miracle he'd become a physiological genius—just his willingness to act as a pure receiver and transmitter for infused knowledge when someone needed help.

Time on the Other Side

A more appropriate title for this section might be "Time Everywhere But Here," since it's primarily on earth that we've come up with the artificial measurement of time and the idea that there's such a thing as "past, present and future." Those concepts are as much of a habit with me as they probably are with you, so I can accept without completely grasping the fact that on the Other Side and throughout the rest of the universe, there's really no such thing as time.

Christians, Jews, Buddhists, Hindus, Muslims, the Ba'hai and countless other worshipers of varying beliefs throughout the world agree that when God created us, He gave us the gift of eternity. (Tiresome skeptics say, "Prove it." I've finally started replying, "You prove we're wrong. We're busy.") Whether that eternity involves one incarnation on earth, as some believe, or many, as I'm convinced beyond all doubt, is beside the point for this conversation. What's essential is the truth of the eternity God promised us—a God who never breaks His promises—and the reality that when it comes to eternity, there is no beginning and there is no end. There is no yesterday, no tomorrow, no "last week" or "an hour from now," no holding up a yardstick to time at all, as if it's a straight line that can be measured.

Instead, in the context of eternity, on the Other Side and throughout the universe, there is only "now." For a visual concept of eternity, a circle is more accurate than a straight line, and the infinity symbol—the best description I can come up with is a figure 8 lying on its side—is more accurate than a circle. A continuum. Always was, always will be. I can give you words upon words upon words about what eternity means, and I'm sure that your faith in the word of God, as devout and certain as mine, will embrace them without question, while your earth-trained mind, like mine, keeps right on trying to imagine it.

Prophets are often as hindered as everyone else by this earthly time versus eternity confusion. On one hand, when prophets receive knowledge of something they know hasn't happened yet, they can obviously put it in the "future" context. Nostradamus, for example, saw the coming of three Antichrists, one from near Italy, one from Germany and one from the Middle East. He also saw some of the circumstances around them and the outcome of their tyranny, which gave him some clues about a general earthly time frame. It's only when

he, his countless translators or some combination of both felt occasionally compelled
to come up with specific years for specific
events that the believers and the nonbelievers in Nostradamus's credibility get to really
square off.

The most recent highly publicized Nostradamus controversy that I'm aware of
(and maybe I should be ashamed to admit
it, but I don't really pay rapt attention to
these things) was the debate over whether
he did or didn't predict the terrorist attack
on the World Trade Center in New York City
on September 11, 2001.

One media quote from a Nostradamus
quatrain read like this:

*In the year of the new century and nine
    months,*
*From the sky will come a great King of
    Terror . . .*
*In the city of York there will be a great
    collapse,*
two twin brothers torn apart by chaos.

But then, hot on the heels of that admit-
tedly chilling passage came another report,
tersely correcting the quote and printing

what Nostradamus *actually* said five hundred years and who knows how many translations later:

> *In the year 1999 and seven months*
> *From the skies shall come an alarming*
>   *powerful king . . .*
> *Two royal brothers shall war so much*
> *one against the other.*

No "new century and nine months," no "twin brothers torn apart," and a "King of Terror" transformed to an "alarming powerful king." So in the sixteenth century Nostradamus apparently said that two royal brothers would be at war and a powerful king would come from the sky in July of 1999, when everyone knows that the real horror, having nothing to do with two royal brothers but twin towers instead, being destroyed from the sky under orders from a terrorist maniac, came a full two years and two months later.

I honestly have no investment whatsoever in whether Nostradamus was right or wrong, legitimate or a fraud. I do have an investment in simply making the point that focusing on the minutiae of information from the Other Side, particularly when it comes to human-made calendar years against a backdrop of God-made eternity, can do a great disservice to the prophets who receive the information and, of far more importance, to their prophecies. When messages originate in a place where everything is "now" and time doesn't even exist, how reasonable is it of us to expect that the messages include absolute accuracy about something we on earth just made up for our own convenience in the first place?

Many prophets, including Edgar Cayce, Madame Blavatsky and Eileen Garrett, have predicted that the lost continents of Atlantis and Lemuria will reemerge someday. Edgar Cayce said Atlantis would begin to rise from the sea in 1968 or 1969. Obviously that didn't happen, although oceanographers made discoveries in those years off the coast of Bimini that some would argue *kind of* supported Cayce's prophecy. But let's say he was wrong. 1968 and 1969 came and went with no Atlantis and no Lemuria. Does it really serve any purpose to throw up our hands and say, "He clearly didn't know what he was talking about, therefore neither do any of the rest of them,

Atlantis and Lemuria probably never existed to begin with, and they're certainly not going to reappear out there in the middle of our oceans, for heaven's sake"? Or doesn't it make just as much sense to respect what's apparently a fairly common vision among several known prophets, that where Atlantis and Lemuria once were they will be again? I think we owe widespread visions at least a strong "maybe" in our eternal lifetimes instead of an arrogant "never," as if we're so much wiser than the spirit world on the Other Side, which passed along those visions to begin with.

(Atlantis and Lemuria will rise again someday, by the way, but I don't want to get too far ahead of myself.)

Sharing Information with the Other Side

Please don't let me give you the mistaken impression that infused knowledge is the only way that prophets and the Other Side interact to "compare notes." In fact, as you know if you've read any of my books or heard me speak for more than about three minutes, we all communicate with the spirit world on the Other Side on a regular basis in many different ways. And since there are no special rules for prophets, their means of gathering information from Home are exactly the same as everyone else's; it's just that prophets tend to receive information with a more specific focus and purpose.

Spirit Guides

Almost every person on earth has a Spirit Guide. (The few exceptions aren't relevant to this conversation, but you can read about them at length in *Life on The Other Side* or *The Other Side and Back.* Look for a chapter called "The Dark Side." Enough said?) Prophets are the rule, not the exception. It's safe to say that every prophet who's ever existed has had a Spirit Guide and that, with or without conscious awareness, the prophet's Spirit Guide has been responsible for at least some of his or her messages from the Other Side.

For those of you who aren't clear on exactly what a Spirit Guide is, the brief explanation goes like this:

Once we've made the decision to take a (relatively) quick trip away from Home for another incarnation on earth, we go through a number of steps to guarantee we accomplish all our goals on this journey. One of those steps is the selection of a Spirit Guide. A Spirit Guide is someone from the Other Side who's incarnated at least once, so they'll have some understanding of life on earth. It's someone who knows every intricate detail of the chart we've written for this particular trip, someone with the wisdom and skill to keep us on track while at the same time letting us fall and get lost and find our way back when we inevitably need to. It's someone who'll be our most devoted companion every moment of every day whether we believe in the guide or not, the constant bridge between us and Home, one of the guide's hands holding ours at all times and the other holding God's.

Our Spirit Guides talk to us constantly. Mine is named Francine. I first began consciously hearing her voice when I was eight years old. I can both hear her and channel her, not only for infuriatingly vague advice about my life (like all Spirit Guides, she insists on making me learn most of my big lessons the hard way) but also for a stunning wealth of information about the Other Side and countless other subjects.

Whether or not you literally hear your Spirit Guide's voice, you can count on it that you're aware of your guide's talking to you, and that you're listening. You've called it "instinct," you've called it "a gut feeling," you've said "something told you" to do or not to do something, you've referred to "just knowing," and I promise you that in about eight out of every ten of those cases, you were actually referring to quiet messages from your Spirit Guide, who is, don't forget, your personal messenger from Home.

And it really is essential to keep in mind that Spirit Guides are exactly that—spirits, residents of the Other Side, living full, busy, blissful lives there while fulfilling their sacred responsibility to us as we slog along here on earth. Like all spirits, they have full access to all universal information and the infinite research and study facilities of Home, including the Akashic Records, with eternity as their frame of reference.

I can tell you from firsthand experience that whenever Francine answers a question in which I try to pin her down about, let's say, how soon I can expect some event to happen, she invariably starts with the words *"By your measurement of time,"* then continues, "it will take [however many months, weeks or years]." The pause before she answers, during which I know she's trying to calculate this inane earthly time thing, always reminds me of me of trying to shop or just pay for a simple meal in any country that doesn't use American currency. No matter how self-assured and sophisticated I try to look as I hand a clerk or waiter a stack of foreign bills, the truth is, I might be giving the person the equivalent of $50,000 for a hamburger for all I know, and telling him or her to keep the extra $100,000 as a tip. It's worth repeating: if the spirit world has a few accuracy problems trying to translate eternity into a time frame, I have no stones to throw.

At any rate, not only is it a guarantee that every prophet had or has a Spirit Guide, it's also a guarantee—a *guarantee*—that many prophecies are the result of direct conscious or subconscious communication between prophets and their Spirit Guides.

Astral Travel

Astral travel is becoming more and more of a mainstream concept, or at least it's not as limited as it once was to a handful of us off-the-wall lunatics. As you probably know, at the core of astral travel is the premise (fact) that the human body is simply the vehicle in which the separate entity called the divine eternal spirit resides during its visits to earth, and that the spirit is able to come and go from that body to travel freely throughout the world, the universe and the glorious familiarity of the Other Side.

It always makes me smile when a client comments in passing that he or she either doesn't believe in astral travel or guesses it makes sense from a theological point of view, but would never want to try it. You should see the looks on clients' faces when I break it to them that, believe it or not, like it or not, they're probably astrally traveling on an average of three or four nights a week while they sleep. They deny it, of course, as if I've accused them of something, but then I start asking them to tell me about their "dreams." Some are chaotic, seeming nonsense, classic release dreams. Others are wish dreams. Still others are problem-solving. (My *Book of Dreams* elaborates on all of those and more, so I won't belabor them here.)

But invariably, sooner or later, clients tell me about a dream that "seemed so real." Often they mention a sensation of flying, or even remember looking down at treetops and the landscape below. And then they talk about finding themselves with a departed loved one, either in some nostalgic setting on earth or in some place more beautiful than they can quite describe, feeling great peace from even the most uneventful time with those loved ones they've missed so much. It's common for them to remark on how the two of them had this wonderful conversation without any actual words being spoken. The "dream" always unfolds in perfect chronological order, with a beginning, middle and end. Finally, there's very often a sudden, sometimes unpleasant sense of falling as it ends, being jolted awake and then needing a few moments to shake off the instant of joy over such a cherished reunion, followed by the crushing realization that it was "only a dream."

Except, of course, it wasn't a dream at

all, it was a classic example of one of the out-of-body astral trips our spirits take, most often while our conscious minds are at rest. Sleep is an ideal time for astral travel, and Francine tells me that all of us astrally visit the Other Side once or twice a week while our bodies are snoring away in their beds. We might go there to visit departed loved ones, or to meditate in the Gardens of the Hall of Justice, or to spend time doing research in the Hall of Records, or just because we're Homesick. Or we might choose to astrally visit some person or place right here on earth instead, or some favorite populated destination in the distant universe. We have that choice, and we make that choice, happily and frequently, whether our conscious minds retain "postcards" from our astral travels or not.

Astral travel is also possible, even fairly common, during hypnosis, meditation, unconsciousness, debilitating illness, coma and near-death experiences. Anytime you hear someone describe looking down at his or her own body, even if the person thinks it was just imagined, it's a safe bet the person is telling you about an astral experience.

Anytime you have the odd feeling that a loved one who's very ill has visited you, even though you know it's impossible, you were undoubtedly right the first time, the loved one did visit, his or her spirit taking a nice astral break from a body and/or conscious mind that were no longer serving the person well. And if you really want to talk to an expert on the subject of astral travel, listen closely to young children as they tell you about their night dreams, their "daydreams" and what they "pretended" while they played. They may not have the vocabulary to articulate it clearly, but astral travel is the primary form of transportation on the Other Side, after all, and to children, newly arrived from there, it's as natural and normal as walking, if not more so.

Again, it's a guarantee that every prophet who's ever lived experienced countless astral trips during his or her "career." It's also a guarantee that during those astral trips, prophets could have traveled to any destination they chose, including the vast maze of aisles in the Hall of Records, the unimaginable wealth of research centers and libraries and laboratories, and even the sacred Akashic Records themselves in the familiar sacred splendor of Home. We'll never know for sure how many prophecies have come as a direct result of astral travel to the Other Side. But when you're in search of answers about the future, why not head straight to that one divine place where all answers can be found, and where the future is transformed into an ever-present "now"?

A Personal Note

All that having been said, I should add before you begin reading my own prophecies, which follow, that I can't be all that precise about the mechanics of how I collect my information. I only consciously consulted my Spirit Guide Francine on rare occasions during this process, to help clarify some point or another. Beyond that, I have no idea how to break down my process into, let's say, X amount of infused knowledge, Y number of unconscious messages from Francine and Z number of personal research trips to the Other Side via astral travel.

It's much like when I'm asked as a psychic how I do what I do. Again, I have no idea. I was born this way, so I'm no better at answering that question than you probably are at explaining how you do those things that have come naturally and easily to you for as long as you can remember. "I just do it" is all I can ever seem to come up with. I'm never trying to be glib or dismissive; I'm just being honest. I suppose I also refuse to let myself even be tempted to do some intellectual step-by-step blueprint of the psychic or prophetic procedure, for fear that if I really start thinking about it I might not be able to do it anymore.

Have you ever had someone ask you about one small detail of something you do all the time with no thought at all? Such as "When you walk, does your left arm swing forward when your right leg takes a step, or when your left leg takes a step?" Or "When you're just standing in one place talking to someone, what do you do with your hands while you're standing there?" Try to notice one of those details so you can come up with an answer, and you'll suddenly walk so awkwardly that you look like a beginner at this walking thing, or become so self-conscious about what your hands are up to while you're talking to someone that your hands suddenly feel as foreign and incomprehensible to you as if you had snowshoes on the ends of your arms.

So no. I have no idea how I do what I do, or exactly how I get my psychic and prophetic information, and I'm not going to think about it. I've been tested a bazillion times by a whole list of psychologists, scientists, paranormal researchers, psychiatrists, hypnotherapists and MDs. Let *them* think about it. I'm busy just doing it.

The one thing I'm crystal clear about, always have been and always will be, is where it all ultimately comes from, and that's God. Whether it's delivered via Spirit Guide or astral travel or infused knowledge, it originated from God, like each one of us and everything else in this universe. I have no more to do with it than to act as a transmitter, and any flaws and errors and miscalculations in everything you're about to read are completely my responsibility. I've been wrong many times before, and I'll be wrong again. According to the tests I mentioned in the previous paragraph, my accuracy rate is somewhere between 87 and 90 percent if

I'm recalling correctly. That's not 100 percent.

Only God can truthfully claim 100 percent.

That disclaimer aside, though, you can rest assured that every prophecy that follows is sincere, honest, from my heart and, to the very best of my knowledge, accurate as of this book's release date in July of 2004.

PART I

THE EARTH

CHAPTER FOUR

✳

The Ecology

Thirty years ago I was in San Francisco, doing an episode of a Bay Area television show called *People Are Talking.* For the life of me I can't remember what someone asked that prompted me to say this, but I know exactly what words came out of my mouth.

"We're starting into a polar tilt," I suddenly announced with all the certainty in the world.

I was about as familiar as you probably are with what a polar tilt is—it's a shift in the angle at which the earth tips on its axis, toward or away from the sun, causing all sorts of changes in the oceans, the weather, the topography, and so on. It was as much of a surprise to me as it was to the show's hosts and the audience, but since these things only come *through* me, not *from* me, it wasn't mine to edit or judge or comment on, it was only mine to give a voice to and then move on.

I still remember my office getting even more calls than usual after that particular show. Most of the calls went something like "Love the psychic stuff, Sylvia, but stay away from science, since you obviously have no clue what you're talking about." Others skipped the compliment and went straight for my throat with "Polar tilt?! You're even crazier than I thought you were!"

Well, I don't know if you've watched the Discovery Channel and the Learning Channel as often as I have in the last few years (and I'm not just claiming I watch them to try to impress you, I'm really a huge fan), but I've seen specials on both channels about changes the earth has been going through because of the polar tilt.

My point being that I'm most definitely not an expert on science, I'm not a scientist at all, I've never been a scientist and I'll never be a scientist. But I'm not a crackpot, either, and when I'm right, I'm right. This poor planet is going through an enormous number of changes. And we can only blame a handful of them on the polar tilt.

Dinosaurs and Asteroids

One of the theories I've heard again and again about the extinction of dinosaurs is that the earth collided with a huge asteroid that, among other things, covered the sun for a very long time. Without the sun, plants died, and without plants to eat, the dinosaurs died.

We do have an asteroid collision in our future, in or around 2021. But don't panic. We're not going to lose a single dinosaur when it hits, or a single human life either. It will come down harmlessly in a remote area of the Southwest, with plenty of warning and brilliant tracking/guidance/deflection by the collaborative efforts of NASA and the United States Air Force.

I mean this: if you're determined to be frightened about some kind of pervasive threat to the future of life on our planet, don't waste another moment looking up, braced to duck from a killer asteroid. Instead, look around, or in the mirror, because we human beings are the most ruthless, relentless threat—and the greatest hope—earth has ever known. Asteroids are just inanimate objects with no brains, no souls and no control whatsoever over where they go or what they do. What in the world is *our* excuse?

You don't need a psychic to tell you about our worldwide pollution problems. You don't need me to remind you that smoke, exhaust, aerosols, massive blasts of missile fuel and countless other human-made gases and pollutants have created a tear in our ozone layer like a giant run in a nylon stocking. The ozone layer is the earth's protective canopy, and without it we get, among other things, a warming trend, which causes glaciers to melt, and a much less filtered exposure to the UV rays of the sun. Again, no news to you, I'm sure.

I can't quite decide if it's amazing or not that over the next five years, until about 2010, we're going to be seeing an alarming rise in skin cancer, especially in children. On one hand, with the ozone layer in so much trouble, it makes sense. On the other hand, with so much media coverage about the harmful effects of UV rays and so many products available to help protect against them, you'd think we'd be too smart and well informed to be that careless. Oh, well. The good news is, if everyone pays attention and takes action, that's one prediction you can pull right out from under me. And I'll be the first to applaud if you do it.

The Rain Forests

"Save The Rain Forests" has been a popular bumper sticker for decades. Sadly, that often means it's long since ceased to have any more impact than bumper stickers announcing what the drivers would rather be doing or what baseball team they like. There's also no question that we all get bombarded every time we turn around or pick up the phone with appeals for donations to save everything from the rain forests to canceled sitcoms, as if they're issues of equal gravity, and we just plain stop listening. In the case of the rain forests, we can't afford to do that anymore.

Tropical rain forests once covered somewhere between 6 and 8 million square miles of this planet. Thanks to fires and our brilliant interpretation of the word "progress," those square miles have now been reduced to less than 4 million. If we keep this up, we might easily have no rain forests at all by 2032.

The question is, since many of us live maybe five thousand or six thousand miles from the nearest rain forest and will probably never even vacation near one, what possible difference could a few less rain forests make?

Or, more to the point of this particular book, what possible difference *will* a few less rain forests make?

Well, first of all, we have to get this whole concept of geographical distance out of our heads when it comes to the rain forests. Whether they're in Asia, the Amazon or Africa, they might as well be home to every one of us; they're as essential to us and the earth as the lungs are to the human body. I don't pretend to understand every detail of photosynthesis. But I know, as you undoubtedly do, that part of it involves plants taking carbon dioxide molecules from the air and releasing oxygen back into the air. I also know that without oxygen, we human beings, and all the other animals on earth, for that matter, will die.

The rain forests may only cover less than 2 percent of the surface of the earth. But more than half of all the plant species on this earth originate in the rain forests. The scope of the worldwide use of those plants in present and future medical and consumable products is both incalculable and, at the same time, almost beside the point. For this discussion it's enough to say that abusing, bulldozing and destroying the world's rain forests amounts to our slowly but surely cutting off our own oxygen supply, i.e., essentially cutting our own throats and calling it "progress."

Because of general public, corporate and political laziness toward preserving and protecting the rain forests between now and around 2012, we're going to see an alarming increase in breathing disorders and diseases, from asthma to emphysema to bronchial infections to pneumonia to countless variations on all of those. Respirators and air purifiers will be as common in the average home as televisions and coffeemakers. Pollution will become much more persistent and widespread, and since it's so visible, it will also get the bulk of the blame for the near-epidemic proportions of those breathing disorders. (Not that pollution isn't despicable, a vicious enemy that's been with us for far too long, and God bless everyone who's joined the nonviolent battle against it.)

But in around 2012 or 2013 a coalition of five major international corporations is going to start looking beyond the pollution problem at the ongoing destruction of the rain forests. They won't "discover" that destroying rain forests weakens the atmosphere and its ability to counteract pollution, while depriving us of oxygen and the other life-giving elements the rain forests naturally manufacture—we already know that. What they will do is combine their almost limitless resources and mobilize a vast, worldwide, ultimately successful movement to revitalize the rain forests. As a direct result of their efforts, we'll see a significant improvement in global air quality and an equally significant decline in the global epidemic of chronic breathing disorders.

The motives behind all these corporate efforts aren't completely selfless. One corporation's CEO has a child with severe chronic asthma, and his billion-dollar investments in the hybrid car industry and saving the rain forests are only a fraction of his understandable efforts to make her well. Another is owned by a tough, no-nonsense man who happens to have complete and total faith in karma. He doesn't necessarily call it karma—he might be more comfortable with "what goes around comes around," or "you reap what you sow." But he's absolutely convinced (and he's right) that this universe God created operates on certain nonnegotiable laws, one of which is karma, and there's no amount of money or big enough gun to make our karmic debt go away. His philanthropic generosity, including the massive corporate resources he pours into the rain forests, boils down to his wanting the "karmic credit." Since he'll get it, and the whole world will benefit from it, who cares what inspired the thought in the first place?

By the way, in case you're wondering— we all know that karma, or "what goes around comes around," is real. Too slow for our liking sometimes, but it's a guarantee, we can count on it, and we're all either blessed with the universal law of karma or cursed with it, depending on our own behavior as we go through this life. And since every town and city, every state and country, and every small business and major corporation is made up of people, each with the karma he or she has created and is creating, it's simple logic that towns, cities, states, countries, small businesses and major corporations have collective karma of their own. We've all seen very public proof of that, both good and bad, and we'll see it again.

To you corporations who'd like to turn your karma around and know perfectly well you need to, whether you've been caught yet or not: please don't feel compelled to wait until 2012 on my account. The rain forests and this planet that can't survive without them could use your help right now.

Acid Rain

I can't even remember how long ago I first started hearing about acid rain as if it might be just a few storms away. Then, as I understood it, any of us who were caught outside in a downpour would suddenly, without warning, simply melt to death, with nothing left of us but a sad, steaming puddle.

It kept not happening, and I stopped listening. But I never forgot about it or quit shuddering a little at the thought of it.

And in 2024 we'll see acid rain as part of an ecological cycle that will change our way of life for decades to come.

Some future mutation of nuclear testing will be a major contributor to this acid rain, as will a lot of well-intentioned space exploration. Oddly, it won't be the rain that sets off alarms in the beginning, it will be a parasite or fungus in the soil that will first be noticed in England, Germany and France. Testing will reveal that this soil pollution was caused by severely polluted rain, which of course won't get any less polluted as it makes its way around the earth. Since nothing healthy can grow from contaminated soil fed by polluted rain, vegetation will be compromised, as will all the animals and humans that eat it, to say nothing of our planet's water supply, on which this same polluted rain will fall.

The late 2020s will be a rough, desperate, survivalist era for us. We'll have to wear protective headgear and clothing in the rain, not to keep us dry but to keep our skin from being badly burned or worse. All food will be human-made, and water will be astronomically expensive after all the purification processes required to bottle it. Birth defects will soar, as will animal mutations, and it will take even more courage and faith in God than we need today to keep going.

I hope I've made it clear in every book I've written what I'm about to point out again now: those who choose to come to this earth in bodies that are physically or mentally challenged, or at a time of war or terrible unrest or grave natural threats, are very special, advanced spirits. It's no coincidence that those spirits happen to be around when this planet most needs them, and that the same will be true in those dark future years of acid rain and poisoned earth.

Domed Cities

Brilliant, compassionate minds intent on the survival of human and animal life in the late 2020s, and on survival with quality, will create and execute the concept of protecting us under towering domes rising high above our cities. Domed cities will first be built in the United States, closely followed by Germany and England. India and the Middle East will be among the slowest to follow suit, as will the Orient, although eventually there will be domes on every continent and in every corner of the world. The domes will be made of some kind of three-ply synthetic glass and plastic composite, more durable than anything we know today. They'll be retractable to allow for air travel, and high enough and clear enough, although tinted for UV protection, to be virtually indiscernible to the population living, working and finally thriving beneath them.

If you've ever been to a greenhouse, hothouse or solarium, you've seen the conceptual basics of domed city living: environmentally controlled, atmospherically filtered and regulated, light and dark on command, all conditions programmed for the maximum health of the species being cultivated inside. Viruses can neither grow nor spread in the purified air, and allergies and other breathing disorders gradually cease to exist, allowing humans and animals to be restored to full health. Plants flourish in lab-detoxified soil, irrigated with clear, safe water, pest-free in this new rarified world that can allow or disallow whatever it chooses.

Which, of course, is part of the problem. As life inside the domed cities becomes healthier and more ideal, it also becomes more crowded. And as it becomes more crowded, stress and resentment inevitably begin to set in, with the ultimate result that those who are deemed to be "less desirable" are exiled to the brutal, unprotected atmosphere outside the domes. Banishment becomes a very popular sentence for criminals. Unfortunately, it also becomes a convenient way for the wealthy to discriminate against the poor, the educated to discriminate against the uneducated and the "valuable" to discriminate against the "useless," as if anyone is more valuable in God's eyes than anyone else.

Some domes do eventually spring up in a few regions of the countryside throughout the world. Many people not only take refuge there but actually form successful communal farms and an incredibly close-knit society, having somehow survived the arid void outside the domes and then nursed themselves and one another back to health when they found their way back inside. Several of them will go on to become the backbone of the reintegrated society later in the millennium, in around 2060, when the earth's atmosphere has healed itself enough for us to venture out of the domes and begin to travel freely on this planet again, having learned from our mistakes— please, God!

Now, we have any number of choices of what we can do with this information. We can hide in our basements for the rest of our lives and pretend that hiding in a basement is worth calling a "life." We can give in to depression and pessimism, stop trying and live with the knowledge that by doing nothing we're contributing to the problem.

Or we can remember that a century ago, in the early 1900s, there were prophecies of not one but two great world wars, more horrible and deadly than anything the earth could have ever imagined, and huge balls of fire would fall from the sky and explode in the midst of our cities, killing our children and poisoning the very air we breathe.

I'm sure it would have sounded so grotesque that we'd have been sure we'd never live through it, or even want to. Well, those prophecies turned out to be absolutely true, and yet here we are, still standing, with more to show and be proud of for these last hundred years than we could possibly list, because in the end God created survivors, not victims, when He breathed life into our eternal spirits.

CHAPTER FIVE

Weather and Topography

I know. Two things we only have a limited amount of control over, but as we established in the previous chapter, we can help. And what we can't do much about, we can at least keep a watchful eye out for. Again, though, please, for God's sake, stop far short of holing up in your basement with a bunch of canned goods for the rest of your life. For one thing, you can't be of any use to yourself or to anyone else while you're down there, so what's the point of sticking around at all? For another thing, if life really gets bad enough to warrant something as drastic as hiding in a hole, imagine how you'll feel when you finally get curious enough to take a look around someday and realize that everyone and everything you cared about is gone anyway. I'll pass, thanks.

Now. Due primarily to the polar tilt and the weakening of the protective ozone layer, this warming trend we're already experiencing hints of will become more and more dramatic, so that by around 2020 it will have reached severe stages. This will cause a kind of microwave oven effect inside the earth—the core of our planet will become red hot and begin emitting steam, creating a rash of volcanic activity around the world and an increase in seismic activity along fault lines, which means that earthquakes will become quite prevalent. The atmospheric dust from these volcanoes and earthquakes will pollute the air and block the sun, causing some disastrous crop failures in the early 2020s.

It will take about five years for things to return to some semblance of normalcy, and during those five years we'll see the good news/bad news effect of near-monsoon rains on the eastern seaboard of North America and throughout South America.

The rains will help moderate the temperatures by a degree or two, but they'll also contribute to the widespread flooding that will be inevitable at around that same time.

If you've traveled to Alaska or anywhere else near the North Pole in recent years like I have, you've undoubtedly been shown the disturbing sight of glaciers melting into the sea right before your eyes. By 2020, when global warming and the polar tilt are at their peak, the glaciers will be nearing extinction, and those massive blocks of ice turning to water will cause worldwide floods, tidal waves and erosion that will alter the coastlines of our continents forever.

Tidal Waves

The most dramatic tidal waves will hit in two completely separate places—the Orient and Florida—during a period between 2025 and 2030.

The tidal waves in the Orient will be an almost monthly phenomenon, with a high number of casualties because the Orient will be slow to adopt the practice of domed population centers.

The Florida tidal waves will be part of a swarm of hurricanes that will batter the southern Atlantic seaboard, particularly in 2028. The survival rate will be spectacularly high, not only because of the protective domed cities that will be underway by then but also because of newly constructed, technologically advanced seawalls. These walls, which we'll start seeing in the early 2020s, will be made of steel, a titanium-like alloy and some other substance that doesn't exist yet that will add an extraordinary resilience so that the walls can bend in gale-force winds and tidal waves without cracking or breaking.

In the late 2030s there will be enormous subterranean volcanic disruptions in the Indian Ocean, causing flooding and tidal waves in bordering countries, particularly Australia and Tanzania. Again, the survival rate will be blessedly high, largely due to the existing technology that will allow enough warning time for people to move inland to high ground.

Plagues and Rivers of Red

With the relentless flooding, particularly on the east coast of North America and throughout South America, we'll see a virtual plague of insects, particularly mosquitoes, flies, roaches and locusts. (Oddly, the thought of tidal waves and floods doesn't bother me nearly as much as this bug thing does. You don't want to be in the same room with me when I see a bug. I just needed to get that off my chest.) At the same time—between about 2022 and 2027—there will be a proliferation of frogs in Central America and the northern third of the South American continent.

Adding to what begins to feel like an onslaught of tabloid headlines coming to life, a system of rivers in the western and southwestern United States that flow into the Gulf of Mexico will turn a deep, dramatic, almost crimson red.

Plagues of locusts and frogs, blood red rivers, on the heels of relentless tidal waves, volcanoes, earthquakes and swarms of hurricanes—it's no wonder widespread rumors of an impending Armageddon will spring up throughout the world, and unfortunately, it's also no wonder that countless phony psychics, gurus and cult leaders will spring up throughout the world right along with those rumors, to make a fast fortune cashing in on the apparent "proof" that Armageddon is upon us.

Except that no, it's not. None of this has anything to do with Armageddon, and if you're around in 2022–2027, I hope you'll make a note to yourself to save your money for something more practical than a dozen anti-Armageddon prayer candles or whatever on earth those despicable swindlers will come up with.

Instead, the "plagues" will be the result of the heat and the slowly receding floodwaters—you couldn't create more ideal conditions for attracting and breeding insects and frogs if you worked at it.

And the rivers of red will come from the underground eruptions and fault-line disturbances in the western United States shaking loose long-buried oxidized (i.e., rust-colored) soil that will simply seep and erode its way into any and all nearby wells, streams and other waterways, eventually feeding into southwestern rivers and giving them a crimson appearance.

So unless this Armageddon we were warned about some two thousand years ago was really just a reference to heat, stagnant water and dirt, I'm prepared to promise you—and I do mean *promise* you—that despite some very impressive "special effects," there is no Armageddon lurking in our immediate future.

Uncommon Showers

We discussed the oncoming blight of acid rain in the "Ecology" chapter, but we didn't discuss another kind of rain we have to look forward to that won't be nearly as insidious. Starting in around 2029, at relatively infrequent intervals, the earth will be subjected to meteor showers. And if there's one adjective that doesn't describe meteor showers, it's insidious—they're about as blatant and overt as a natural disaster can be.

Of course, it's not as if this planet hasn't been in collisions with meteors and meteorites before. But when our atmosphere was at its peak of health, they would be ten times larger until they crashed through the ozone layer and into our "airspace," at which point they would disintegrate for the most part before they reached the earth's surface. In 2029 that won't be the case. The ozone layer and our atmosphere will be considerably weakened by then, and meteor showers will do considerably more damage to our plant life and our topography. Luckily, loss of human and animal life will be minimized by the proliferation of domes, which will have the built-in strength and heat resistance to withstand that much impact and more.

We also have four more comets to look forward to in the next eighty years, passing close enough to the earth that they'll be every bit as spectacular as the Hale-Bopp comet was a few years ago. But please. Please. I'm begging you. Listen to me. Comets are beautiful. They put on a spectacular show. But they are *not* a divine signal of an impending Armageddon, and they're most certainly not a sacred chariot of some kind, arriving to deliver those spirits who are "in on the secret" to their rightful

place by God's side, if they'll just kill themselves and catch the comet on time. I can't
believe it's even necessary to say that, but
everyone who remembers the tragedy of
the Heaven's Gate choreographed suicides
understands that apparently it is. God has
far more efficient ways of bringing us
Home, as we're all well aware, and He will
never, *ever* give us orders to take our own
lives, directly or through anyone else, no
matter how powerful or prophetic or "chosen" that person claims to be.

At any rate, now that I've vented a little
more of my rage against cult leaders, back
to Uncommon Showers. I don't know if
you've ever had a personal, one-on-one
conversation with an experienced astro-
naut, but I've had that pleasure. And I'll
never forget his confiding to me with some
sad dismay that the earth's outer atmosphere has become a veritable junkyard,
thanks to our multinational determination to
explore the universe and our lack of determination to pick up after ourselves while
we're up there.

So it's not just an occasional meteor
shower we have to look forward to, starting

in 2029. Some of our own trash and debris is going to come back to haunt us as well, and for that we're going to have nothing but our own carelessness to thank.

Topographical Consequences

I mentioned earlier that as a result of all this flooding and volcanic and seismic activity, the coastlines of our continents and island nations will be altered and/or "resculpted." I want to clarify that, because I don't see anything as cataclysmic as other prophecies I've read.

✳ I do *not* see the state of California crumbling into the Pacific Ocean along the San Andreas Fault, and I swear it's not just because I happen to live here. There will be ongoing erosion, as there always has been. And previously unknown fault lines will quake their way into the headlines as they literally "let off steam" from surrounding underground eruptions and other earthquakes in the mid-2020s. But a time will never come when either central California or Nevada is beachfront property.

✳ I *do* see some significant loss of land along the coastlines of the Pacific Northwest and Hawaii, due to volcanic eruptions above and under the earth's surface. Again, though, I'm not talking about losses that will extend hundreds of miles inland, but dozens of miles at most.

✳ I also see powerful tsunamis hitting large portions of Japan in around 2026. It's interesting—as a result of these tsunamis, we may see a large new land mass emerging among the Hawaiian islands. I'm sure you'd like something more absolute, but that's as definite as I can get on that subject for now.

✳ I do *not* see a devastating crumbling away of the British Isles. Severe flooding, yes, particularly in the early to mid-2020s, as global warming takes its firmest hold and the glaciers disintegrate into the sea at an unprecedented rate. But when the floodwaters eventually recede, the British Isles will be a bit frayed around their glorious edges but generally intact as ever.

And finally . . .

✳ When the dust clears and the feverish chaos of the Atlantic and Indian Oceans finally breaks by the middle of the twenty-first century, I absolutely believe we'll find ourselves gazing in awe at the reemerged wonders of Atlantis and Lemuria.

CHAPTER SIX

✳

Space Travel:
Ours and Theirs

I'm taking a nice deep breath before I start this chapter, because this is one of several in this book that are bound to make some of you say, "This woman's even crazier than I thought."

Oh, well. It can't be helped. I'll be deciding what to wear to my sixty-eighth birthday party when this book comes out, which means I've been psychic for that same amount of time and exposing myself in public about it for more than half a century. I made some promises to my beloved Grandma Ada before I gave my first reading or stepped onto a stage for the first time: no matter what the subject matter—psychic, spiritual, prophetic, clairvoyant, you name it—I would never lie or deliberately deceive people in any way, I would take full responsibility for saying what I believe in my heart and soul to be the truth no matter how much skeptics might laugh, and I'd be the first to point it out when I was wrong. Nowhere in those promises did the words "play it safe" come up. And at almost sixty-eight, you can bet I'm not about to start now.

So disagree if you like. In fact, don't take my word for anything. I'd much prefer you study and research and read everything you can get your hands on about every subject that interests you and then reach your own well-thought-out, well-informed conclusions. But never let it enter your mind that I have the slightest doubt about anything I'm telling you, because that will never happen. If I'm not sure of something, I'll make that clear. If I state something as an absolute certainty, it's because I believe each and every word of it, or you wouldn't find it in this book.

Now. All that having been said—why we keep bracing ourselves for extraterrestrials to land on earth I have no idea, because they're already here.

The Extraterrestrials Among Us

Before we even start a discussion about extraterrestrials living among us, we need to start getting rid of that distinction between "them" and "us." Let's put it this way: in the context of the infinite, eternal universe, earth is an infant among the planets. And in the context of all the species God created for our spirits to inhabit in this infinite, eternal universe, human beings are infants as well. Extra-terrestrials are just us, spirits created by God. They live the majority of their lives on the Other Side, exactly as we do, and simply happen to take the form of older species on older planets when they incarnate.

Their technology is far more advanced than ours. Their levels of scientific, sociological and spiritual sophistication are far more advanced than ours. Their proficiency at space travel makes us look like talented, earnest beginners. It's not because they're weird, robotic freaks with brains the size of beach balls, and it's not because they're inherently better or smarter or more gifted than we are. It's only because the species they incarnate to has been around longer and has simpler, more elevated priorities than humans, and because these spirits have progressed along their eternal journey of learning at an accelerated rate.

While they're incarnated and visiting us from other planets, we call them extraterrestrials. When they're at Home in the spirit world, we know them as Mystical Travelers, and it's no wonder we're in awe of them.

Mystical Travelers

When most spirits incarnate, we come to earth again and again and again to accomplish what we need to accomplish, continue our eternal search for wisdom and be a loving, generous credit to our Creator.

Mystical Travelers have essentially "graduated" from incarnating on this planet and said to God, "Anywhere in this universe you need me, I'll willingly go." They're extraordinarily powerful spirits, wise, evolved, brilliant and compassionate, going for their

Ph.D.s while the rest of us are still struggling through the rough undergraduate work we call life on earth. They volunteer to incarnate on any inhabited planet, for as short or long a time as their chart demands, just as our incarnations here last no longer than our charts demand, and while none of us is "better" in God's eyes than anyone else, there's no question that Mystical Travelers are His most courageous, most advanced creations.

It's hard to describe a Mystical Traveler on earth except to say that you know one when you see one. For example, I had the honor—and that's the only word for it—of sharing a *Larry King Live* appearance last year with a child named Mattie Stepanek. Mattie was thirteen years old at the time, and in less than five minutes it was obvious that I was in the presence of a Mystical Traveler. I'm sure most of you are familiar with him, but for the few of you who aren't, he's been writing poetry since he could talk, he's published five best-selling books of poetry, he performs tenth- and eleventh-grade-level work and is a part-time student at a local community college. He also happens to have mitochondrial myopathy, a genetic muscular disorder that took the lives of his three siblings. He's in a wheelchair and dependent on a ventilator and supplemental oxygen, and he survived a near-death experience that allowed him to say on *Larry King Live* with a radiance I'll never forget, "I'm afraid of dying, but I'm not afraid of death." Mattie Stepanek knows more about theology and philosophy and peace and humanity and Angels and the relationship between humankind and God than almost anyone else I've ever met. At thirteen years old. Now, that's a Mystical Traveler. (And by the way, he's been named the 2004 Muscular Dystrophy Association National Goodwill Ambassador. Congratulations, Mattie. They're blessed to have you.)

Come to think of it, another Mystic Traveler whose brief presence left an indelible touch of added grace to my life was also a child, this one only four years old when he was stricken with leukemia. (No coincidence that they should both be children with terrible illnesses. Like I said, these are the bravest, most advanced spirits in the universe.) His name was Jared, and he was the son of my friend Oona, who lives in

Kenya. From the moment he was born, everyone commented on what a happy baby he was, but they'd always add adjectives like "serene" and "loving" and "full of light." Even when leukemia took hold of his tiny body, we almost felt as if Jared was using what little energy he had to comfort Oona, as hard as she tried to be strong and brave and comfort and care for him instead. The more time she spent at his bedside, whether they spoke or not, the more she felt he was teaching her about God and the peace that comes from absolute faith in eternity. Even with death on its way, not once was Jared afraid, and there were times when he would open his huge eyes, look directly into hers and smile. Just smile. And in that smile, even though her heart was breaking, she could see that he knew exactly where he was going, and he was ecstatic about the journey.

One morning shortly after Jared's fifth birthday, Oona was standing beside his bed when a sudden certainty flooded through her that he was slipping away, and that she was now spending her last moments with him on this earth. She quietly slid into the bed beside him to hold him. He managed to shift his head just enough to bring his mouth close to her ear, and she barely heard him whisper, "I'm going to God now, Mama. Please hold my hand."

She reached for his hand, and the instant she closed hers around it she literally felt his spirit lift from his body. Her awe from that sensation was only beginning to overtake her when, impossibly, she felt his tiny hand, still holding hers, pull her spirit from her body right along with his.

Rather than taking her to the very real, very tangible tunnel that was waiting for him just above his body, this Mystical Traveler spirit held on to his mother's hand and flew with her through the night sky into a sea of stars, scattered like a million diamonds on black velvet for as far as she could see. Her son's face, full of joy, turned to her in the middle of the universe and said, so clearly she can still hear his voice today, "I just wanted to show you the stars before I go Home."

And then, from somewhere among the stars, a gold-white light appeared and began to grow, almost blindingly brilliant, sparkling, perfect love and wisdom, where that child belonged. From the core of the light, several beings started toward them, too backlit for Oona to make out any of their features. But she knew with a quiet, comforting peace that these graceful beings were coming to welcome her son, and that it was time to let him go. She looked into his eyes one more time, and he smiled back.

"Thank you for coming this far with me, Mama," he said. With that he squeezed her hand and let go, and she felt her spirit slam back into her body on that small bed in that small room, still holding the lifeless hand of her son.

She gently let go, kissed his forehead and whispered back, "Thank you, Jared."

Jared, in his five short years on earth, taught his mother well. Since that day, Oona has devoted her life to the spiritual enrichment of others, hoping to give them at least a glimpse of the brilliant light of divine faith that Jared gave her. It's working. She's an inspiration, changing lives with a serene certainty that reminds me of her son. But if you want to find yourself with a real fight on your hands, try telling her that those moments with Jared among the stars, when she watched God welcome him Home, were a grief-induced hallucination.

She knows what she saw and what she experienced.

So do I.

So do many of you.

Because Mystical Travelers have had incarnations throughout the universe and incarnated here again when we needed them, they are, in a way, one very wise, truly exquisite kind of extraterrestrial among us on this planet.

Others are travelers too, mystical or ordinary but still with a several aeons' head start on us, just visiting, exploring, teaching and fitting in perfectly, as they have been since they first noticed the existence of life on this new creation called earth.

Our History, in Brief, with Extraterrestrials

Yes, extraterrestrials really have been among us since humankind's most ancient times. It's true. And the "rumors" about their connections to everything from the Egyptian and Peruvian pyramids to Stonehenge to the statues of Easter Island are simply fact.

I've listened to more than my share of lectures by "experts" and read more than my share of books on how the Great Pyramids were "really" built. What most of those explanations ultimately boil down to when it's all said and done is "Anything but extraterrestrials." For reasons I'll never understand, many people, some of them brilliant and very well educated, would rather think the pyramids were built by all the stones skipping across Egypt like schoolgirls and then leaping on top of one another one by one than believe they were a collaboration between human beings and extraterrestrials.

Again, I'm in favor of everyone forming their own informed opinions, I just hate to see the extraterrestrials deprived of so much credit where it's most certainly due.

How Extraterrestrials Get Here

It's sad, really, that the tabloids have made such a mockery of light orbs in the sky with trailing lights behind them. Needless to say, the vast majority of those tabloid photos are as phony as a million-dollar bill, or common strobe glares, or flaws on the negatives. Which makes it almost impossible to tell the phonies from the rare occasions when those orbs, some of them white and some of them in pulsating colors, are actually extraterrestrial transports, hurtling toward earth much faster than the speed of light.

Gradually over the next ten or eleven years, through about 2015, these transports are going to be more and more apparent. They'll become less possible to dismiss, even by the most cynical skeptics and secretive government agencies, especially when commercial satellites and communication towers begin picking up discernible patterns of interference and garbled signals.

The transports will land safely and deliberately in deserted areas, primarily Death Valley, the Mojave Desert and the oceans. They're also well aware how to use the unique vortex of the Bermuda Triangle as a chute to come and go completely undetected.

The excitement over the increasingly frequent orb sightings, the growing number of mysterious signals and the discovery of unexplainable debris in the western deserts will hit its stride in about 2012, and an excited search for extraterrestrials, dead or alive, will begin.

The Search for Extraterrestrials

Among those watching the worldwide search for extraterrestrials will be the thousands upon thousands of extraterrestrials who are already here. They've been here for decades, unobtrusive, as ordinary-looking as your next-door neighbor, hard at work in areas in which their advanced knowledge can make a contribution without calling disruptive, counterproductive attention to themselves. They're scientists, they're researchers, they're space engineers, they're nuclear physicists and teachers and botanists and politicians and geologists— they're anything but conspirators in efforts that might promote conflicts, deaths among innocents and wars.

The idea of extraterrestrials coming to earth to either abduct us and perform excruciating, unspeakable experiments on us or to just annihilate us is great if you want to make movies. Logically, it's inane. Any beings sophisticated enough to get here from gigazillions of miles away have the technology to annihilate us without even bothering to land, if annihilation is their goal. And if they're that advanced, they already gathered all the information they needed about our species a few thousand years ago, not to mention the fact that they've probably figured out how to conduct painless experiments by now.

At any rate, the search for extraterrestrials will ultimately end in around 2018, not because we humans cunningly root them out but because they begin stepping forward and identifying themselves to various international organizations and heads of state, particularly the United Nations, NATO, Scotland Yard, NASA and a summit being held at Camp David. These are men and women who are highly visible and widely respected in their various fields—there's even a Nobel Prize winner among them—and their claims about their origins are initially greeted with a combination of disbelief, confusion, embarrassment, hilarity and outrage. As more and more and still more of them come forward, it becomes more and more and still more difficult to dismiss them, particularly when their reputations are so invariably impeccable.

Finally, thousands and thousands of them, with their full cooperation, are isolated, almost quarantined, somewhere in western Europe, closely guarded and subjected to a battery of psychological and biological tests, which will confirm that whatever species they are, it's not one that earth is familiar with.

And then, of course, the real dilemma begins. It's our knee-jerk reaction to banish them immediately to wherever it is they came from—Andromeda and the Pleiades is the most specific information I'm able to get about that. They're strange, after all, undocumented, untraceable, biologically incomprehensible and very possibly a threat to our safety and security. On the other hand, even we aren't foolish enough to easily let go of such obviously valuable and advanced intelligence, especially when our own psychiatric profiles don't detect a hint of aggression or potential malice in them.

In the end, sometime in the early 2020s,

an accord between us and the extraterrestrials is reached. We slowly but surely open our minds to the infinite amount of information they have to offer, not only about distant galaxies in the distant universe we haven't begun to dream of yet but also about the history of our own planet, much of which their ancestors witnessed and toiled over and helped shape. The more our discomfort with them subsides, the more apparent it becomes that they refuse to participate in any political or financial agenda, and the more our trust in them grows, the more freely they begin to travel back and forth from their various planets to ours, so that by around 2060 the sight of extraterrestrial arrivals and departures will be of no more interest than the sight of passing airplanes is to us now.

Our Travels in Space

Again, brilliant and gifted as the minds in the space programs on this planet are, they're still relative beginners in the context of universal technology. The extraterrestrials among us are *not* going to hand us the keys to spaceships that can take us from here to Pluto in sixty seconds or less, any more than you'd take a child who's mastered a bicycle and instantly turn him loose with a Harley-Davidson motorcycle. From the beginning they've been here to gently help and encourage us, not to simply tell us everything they know and deprive us of the process of working for it, struggling, failing, trying again, learning from our mistakes and ultimately succeeding.

And we'll do all of those things before we're through.

* There won't be a successful manned exploration of Mars until around 2012, after one disastrous misstep leading up to that, rushed into action for political reasons and therefore doomed to fail.
* The Mars exploration that succeeds will be a collaboration of four nations, and some of the technology used will be revealed a decade later to have been introduced by extra-terrestrial physicists on the NASA "leg" of the team.
* Chartered moon junkets will become

available in the late 2030s. Extraterrestrials, who will be "out of the closet" on earth by then, will be instrumental in helping with the design of the ships themselves.

✳ A moon base will be created by the early 2040s for tourist visits and as a stopping place for further sightseeing trips within our solar system.

✳ Along with a team of the earth's astronauts and an interfaith council from around the world, extraterrestrials will begin teaching present and future civilian passengers on space travel junkets, and in the process a rapt global audience, about the sanctity and vulnerability of this blessed, torn little planet through the eyes of a traveler in search of a home. The result will be a stunning wave of spiritual unity across previously impenetrable international boundaries.

✳ In around 2080 we'll have exploratory devices on all but one of the planets in our solar system, but not in this century will we exceed the boundaries of our own planetary "neighborhood."

Sometimes it really does take an outsider to help us appreciate what we've got. In our case, it's taken extraterrestrials from all the way across the universe, time and time and time and time again.

But since we and they share the same Creator, and some of us are bound to be Mystical Travelers sooner or later, chances are we'll be able to return the favor some-day.

PART II

SOCIETY'S LANDSCAPE

CHAPTER SEVEN

Politics and the Economy

I want to make a promise to you before this chapter gets started: I'm going to do my best to keep my own political opinions to myself and be as objective as possible on this particular subject. And you know how good I am at that.

There. Now. Moving right along.

Until around the year 2020, the political structure in the United States will remain as it is now, with the Democrats, the Republicans, the Independent party and various other splinter groups vying for majority control of our three current branches of government (executive, judicial and legislative).

Between now and then, we're in for a difficult, disruptive era in our nation's history. The long-term effect will be a positive one, that's a guarantee. We'll just find ourselves needing frequent reminders of that fact along the way, because it's going to look pretty dismal and confusing from time to time.

A president elected sometime after 2008 will die in office of a heart attack. The vice president in line to finish his term will have the unpopular and terribly mistaken intent to declare war on North Korea, which by then actually will possess weapons of mass destruction. In the midst of his unsuccessful efforts to rally congressional and international support for a declaration of war, he'll be assassinated.

The investigation into the assassination will be worldwide in scope, full of cover-ups and a lot of both pleasant and unpleasant surprises. A massive amount of attention will become focused on one of the investigative congressional committees and dark accusations having to do with mishandling funds. In the end it will be revealed that these accusations are part of a conspiracy to erode the American people's faith in their government, with the media used as an unwitting, easily manipulated accomplice to help fan the flames, and the committee will be vindicated.

Both the FBI and the CIA will undergo changes in leadership and structuring, which will result in both organizations, separately and together as a cooperative entity, realizing their full potential, particularly in the anti-terrorism atmosphere that continues to become stronger and more solidified throughout the country and the world. Scotland Yard in particular becomes one of our intelligence community's closest, most valuable allies in our ultimate victory against these ruthless but doomed terrorist cells.

The FBI, the CIA, the Secret Service and special units of the armed forces will also hone their considerable skills by tracking and apprehending key members of three separate antigovernment extremist organizations within the United States between the years 2010 and 2016. One group will be centered in Montana, one will have its headquarters in the Deep South and one will be uncovered in the Colorado Rocky Mountains. They'll use God and the First Amendment as excuses for a series of murders and a lightning-fast computer virus that saturates hard drives and airwaves with supremacist propaganda. A few elected government officials will be exposed and prosecuted as infiltrators from these groups, and the groups' antigovernment intentions will come to have exactly the opposite effect on the American people and instill a fresh new wave of nationalist pride and protective patriotism.

Along the way we'll begin to examine our vulnerabilities, our shortcomings and our government's areas of excess and inefficiency. This will lead to a restructuring of the way our government is organized.

The New Structure of Government

By about 2020 we'll see the end of the one-man presidency and the costly, seemingly perpetual cycle of presidential campaigns and elections. Instead, our executive branch will be essentially phased out and absorbed into the legislative branch, and it's through the legislative branch that we'll exercise our democratic process. The legislature will be considerably streamlined to a body of elected representatives, an equal number from each state of the union, vaguely resembling the ancient Roman senate. Rather than Democrats, Republicans, Independents, etc., the legislature, aka the Senate, will be divided into two groups, the Liberals and the Conservatives, who will sit literally, not figuratively, on opposite sides of a long aisle.

Proposed laws will have to first be submitted and work their way through a series of screening committees. When they're finally presented to the Senate by the committees, they will be debated and either pass or fail by majority vote, and every session of the Senate will be nationally televised.

The New Senate

The elected senators from each state will be an equal balance of men and women. Qualifications for consideration as a nominee will include:

* thirty-five years of age minimum
* U.S. citizen by birth or naturalization
* no criminal record/"clean" background check

* "clean" weekly drug and alcohol screens, which nominees consent to submit to throughout their term in the Senate
* ten years' minimum "clean" independently audited tax returns
* no past or present salaried position with any company that has ever had or might ever have a professional or contractual connection to federal, state or local government
* no past or present membership in any club or organization with lobbyists on salary or retainer
* a signed waiver permitting biannual audits of all expense reports and bank accounts during their Senate term

Wouldn't you love to know how many of our current senators and members of the House of Representatives could qualify— oh, wait, sorry, that was starting to sound nonobjective of me, wasn't it? Never mind.

Senate terms will be limited to eight years, with elections staggered in such a way that only half the Senate is replaced and inexperienced in any given election year. A separate, independent nine-person judiciary panel will be in sole charge of occasional impeachment efforts, and the panel will have the full cooperation of the FBI, the CIA and the Secret Service to investigate all accusations that could lead to impeachment. If the allegations against the senator in question prove true, the results will be both impeachment and criminal charges. If the allegations prove false, another interesting law that actually becomes a national statute in around 2014 might apply.

In around 2014, a law will be passed stating that if anyone accuses another person of a felony and it can be proven that the accuser knew the accusation was false, the accuser can be made to serve the sentence the person he or she falsely accused would have served if convicted. For example, if a woman falsely accuses a man of rape, and it's established beyond a reasonable doubt that the rape never happened, that woman can find herself facing a typical rapist's jail term. Or if, in a particularly ugly divorce case, one parent makes false claims of child abuse against the other in an effort to obtain custody of the children, and it's proved beyond a reasonable doubt that those claims were a deliberate lie, the parent making the false claims can receive a prison sentence comparable to a minimum sentence for felony child abuse.

And so by around 2020, if a senator is subjected to impeachment proceedings that the judiciary panel determines to be based on deliberately false allegations, for purely political reasons, those who initiated the allegations could find themselves impeached and/or in federal prison serving a term appropriate to whatever accusations they manufactured. The long-term effect, in the Senate and in society in general, will be to finally make people much more responsible about the charges they file against one another and the nightmarish ordeals they sometimes put one another through for no other reason than meanness, revenge or greed.

Laws and Legislative Power

State and local governments will be smaller mirror images of the Senate, equally divided between Liberals and Conservatives, men and women, all elected, but with shorter, three-year terms. Their power is more limited in 2020 than it is in 2004, as the new wave of national patriotism and the novelty of the restructured federal government inspire the balance of trust to shift heavily to Washington, D.C. For the first several years of the Senate, state and local governments essentially take a "let's not knock it till we've tried it" approach to these United States being run "by committee."

Sooner or later the Senate will be responsible for voting the following into law:

* The flat tax. Previous presidential administrations will try to make the flat tax a reality. Between Congress, special interest groups, the usual bureaucracy and more behind-the-scenes machinations than we can imagine, it won't happen until the Senate passes it into law as one of its first legislative decisions.
* Generous tax bonuses given to those with careers in the arts, education, law enforcement and public service.
* The official observance of all major holidays celebrated by all major religions in this country. Banks, govern-

ment offices, schools, and so on will be closed in honor of Jewish and Muslim holidays, for example, just as they are in honor of Christmas, and the observances will help familiarize Americans with the traditions of all faiths. There will also be a national Day of Remembrance for Holocaust survivors, victims and their descendants.

✳ Any drug or alcohol offense, from the first offense on, will be punishable not by incarceration but by a minimum of one month of in-patient rehabilitation, detox, medical testing for chemical and physiological imbalances, and psychiatric therapy. If a vehicle is involved in the offense, it will be seized and auctioned to help defray the rehab expenses.

✳ Any male pedophile who's proved guilty of sexual contact with or molestation of a child by DNA and/or any other concrete, irrefutable evidence will be either chemically or surgically castrated as a mandated part of his sentencing. Female pedophiles will undergo a mandated form of chemically induced hormonal "neutering."

✳ Parents found guilty beyond a reasonable doubt of child abuse or neglect or chronic lack of supervision or responsibility for their child's chronic truancy will have several punishments to look forward to. First, they'll lose their children, not to any random foster home or group home that will have them but to one of a vast network of brilliantly run, privately funded facilities throughout the country, staffed by the nation's finest educators, child psychologists, athletic directors, art and music teachers, guidance counselors, and so on. Second, while their children are away making up for lost time, attention and schooling, the parents will take private and group parenting classes. They'll perform a generous number of hours of community service, their photos will appear in the local newspapers and they'll be under strict curfew, while all their home entertainment equipment is held securely for them by the police for the duration of their sentence. Failure to comply with all of these conditions will result in immediate incarceration. Above all, every possible measure will be taken to see to it that it's the parents, not the children, who take the brunt of the punishment for bad parenting, while the children are busy being educated, cared for, disciplined and given a sense of worth and direction.

✳ Capital punishment will become a national mandate rather than a state-by-state decision. There will have to be one guilty verdict, or more, of first-degree murder with special circumstances, with irrefutable forensic evidence of guilt and unanimous psychiatric agreement that the defendant is legally sane and responsible for his or her actions. The death penalty can never be imposed on any defendant under the age of twenty-five. The appeals process in these cases will be given a three-year limit, and barring reversals and/or victories in the appellate courts, the sentence of execution must be carried out within five years of the day the sentence is handed down.

✳ A public health system will be instituted by the Senate that, imagine this, benefits the well-being of Americans as much as or more than it benefits pharmaceutical and insurance companies.

✳ Animal testing under any circumstances for any purpose will be declared intolerable and illegal for the protection of all species, punishable by incarceration and severe fines.

✳ Elementary schools will be required to teach a minimum of one other language besides English, as well as classes in other cultures and traditions around the world.

✳ The Senate will become increasingly involved in broadcasting through the FCC. They'll closely monitor television programming and insist more and more on educational, informative and inspirational shows as opposed to pure entertainment. Their intentions will look good on paper, but the American public will be deeply offended by the concept of government-controlled television in a democracy. Not for the first time, movements will be initiated throughout the country to modify the structure of the federal government and return some lost power to state and local governments. The modifications will ultimately succeed, but the Senate won't relent without a struggle after enjoying an imbalance of power in their favor for longer than is healthy in any democratic system.

A Few Words About the Economy

And I do mean "a few."

The year 2020 will spark an amazing resurgence in the popularity of the barter system throughout the United States, with goods and services almost becoming a more common form of payment than cash as people try to regain their trust in the economy.

We become much more self-sufficient as individuals and as a nation, insisting on providing our own basic necessities and bringing our companies and our jobs back home. It's not so much an isolationist period as it is a period of economic and government restructuring. We'll turn into an interesting combination of a society whose technology is progressing at almost breakneck speed and, at the same time, a society that's redeveloped and improved on our passion for growing our own food, sewing our own clothing and building our own furniture and houses.

The most conspicuous changes we'll see economically by 2020 are the end of IRAs, mutual funds, pension and retirement plans and the stock market. I simply wanted to mention it so you can't say I didn't warn you. As for what it implies about the deficit by then, I'll leave that to you to draw your own conclusions.

Our Place in the World

We Americans are, as a whole, compassionate, brave, intelligent, strong, proud, resilient, optimistic, generous, God-loving people. The fact that many other countries around the world would have far less flattering adjectives for us is sad, undeniable and, in some ways, understandable.

Gradually, over the next couple of decades, our image in the world's eyes will improve. What's most interesting is that we'll make the greatest strides in gaining, or regaining, international respect by shifting the majority of our focus back on ourselves and finally addressing our own problems head-on until we solve them.

We passionately believe that democracy is the finest, fairest form of government on earth, and it is. We're exactly right to cherish our freedom, to protect it and to take pride in it. Even when our restructured Senate gets carried away with itself in the early 2020s, it won't hold a candle to the rigid governmental control we'll see in parts of Europe, Asia and Africa by then. And in fact, for several years during the 2020s, the most liberal democracy on earth will be Australia, which will attract so many immigrants that it will actually have to close its borders for a brief period of time.

What we in America will start working on in earnest, particularly by around 2009 or 2010, is those undeniable "buts" that we and the rest of the world are all too aware of as communication makes the global community smaller and smaller by the day.

"Our system *works*," we proudly announce. *But . . .*

* not all of our children are fed, clothed, educated, protected from harm and medically cared for
* not all of our population has a place to live
* not all of our youth get more attention from positive role models than they do from gangs and drug dealers
* not all of our willing and available workforce can find jobs
* not all of our elderly are protected from harm or properly cared for either financially or medically
* not all of our death-row inmates are guilty
* not all of our elected officials and major corporations consider the welfare of our people to be a higher priority than the size of their personal bank accounts

The list of "buts" goes on and on. So, thank God, does our list of resources to address every one of them when we set our minds to it.

And that resolve is coming, mark my words. It won't take a firm, visible hold until a few years from now, when our current confusion and sense of frustrated vulnerability begin to settle and we start tending to our own long-neglected wounds. We can't and won't live up to our greatest potential as "one nation, under God" until we've inspired the world, not by sheer brute force but by example, as we have before and will again, that "liberty and justice for all" really means something in these United States.

CHAPTER EIGHT

*

Religion

There aren't subjects much nearer or dearer to my heart and soul than religion, and I want that to be crystal clear. Any group whose earnest intention is to reinforce, honor and celebrate our divine connection to the loving, eternal God who created us has my profound respect. The fact that I don't always appreciate the way we humans let dogma, politics, greed and grandstanding overshadow that intention doesn't diminish my profound respect for religion itself in the least.

And it's dogma, politics, greed and grandstanding—all human-made, not God-made, I can't stress that enough—that are going to be making some significant and healthy changes in our future relationships with our respective religions. *Not with God.* Just with the religions through which we express our specific beliefs, our love for Him and our thanks.

Two major changes in the religious world will have a far-reaching emotional ripple effect. The first will occur in the Catholic Church. After Pope John Paul II passes away, there will only be one more elected Pope. He will be succeeded by what is essentially a triumvirate of popes, or a college of cardinals, who will collectively share the responsibilities of all previous popes. The second change, sometime between 2015 and 2018, will be a kind of Christian congress, a cooperative unity of Protestant faiths in the interest of accomplishing long-term worldwide goals.

The spiritual inspiration these two changes trigger, which neither the Catholics nor the Protestants will particularly see coming but that both will benefit from enormously, will come from the underlying message that if strength in numbers is more responsive to current realities than tradition is, then maybe strength in numbers needs to become the new tradition. It's a simple fact that our spirits know the truth when they hear it, and words like "united" and "collectively share" and "cooperative" used in the same sentence with "God" resonate in our souls far more than even the most gorgeous traditions ever will.

As for the idea that traditions are sacrosanct and should never be forfeited for the sake of change no matter what, by the way, all I can say is, if that were true we'd still be sacrificing animals and virgins and flogging blasphemers in the town square. Please.

Again, the strength in numbers concept, either inspired by or simply exemplified by the adjustments at the head of the Catholic and Protestant churches, will reflect itself in a far more general way by around 2025, when more of a communal mind-set takes hold among the faithful of all major religions, far beyond just Catholics and Protestants. I'm not talking about isolated religious communities "For Members Only," which have often been historically ruled by arbitrary mandates, fear and an unhealthy sense of superiority and elitism in comparison to society in general. Instead, this God-inspired communal mind-set will consist of more and more people being unified by their individual searches for more depth and substance in their relationships with their Creator. These are not people who are rejecting their respective religions, which they feel have given them the history, foundation and momentum of their beliefs. They're simply people who want to take their religious beliefs and propel them both deep within themselves and far out into the world.

Religion Collaborates

So in approximately 2025 all religions of the world that choose to participate, which will include most of them except for a few ultraconservative and ultraseparatist sects, will join forces and funds for the good of one another, the community of humankind and themselves. What's extraordinary is, with no one denomination or religion jockeying for position and/or its own agenda, this collaboration works, in very tangible, gratifying ways.

In an increasing number of cities, states, provinces and countries throughout the globe we'll see what will become known as "Healing Centers" springing up. They'll be beautiful clusters of four pyramid-shaped buildings, each adorned with glistening, rotating crystals at their peak. The compounds will be relatively small, so that even the farthest perimeters will be within easy walking distance of one another and always, *always* wheelchair accessible. The grounds will be exquisitely but simply landscaped with low-maintenance indigenous plants and a wealth of reflecting pools, meditation benches and waterfalls.

Because they will be truly interfaith and a cooperative of various religions coming together to benefit humankind, nothing more, nothing less, Healing Centers will offer a vast array of services from a vast array of disciplines, as well as many services rooted in just plain common kindness and decency.

One of the four pyramid-shaped buildings of the compound will be exclusively devoted to around-the-clock food, clothing, shelter, shower and other basic grooming facilities, medical care, crisis and emergency counseling—anything people for whatever reason are unable to provide for themselves. The building will be completely staffed by volunteers, from the cooks to the doctors to the counselors to the maintenance crew, and the supplies are donated—the food, clothing, bedding, shower and grooming basics, first-aid equipment, and so on—all of this from the collective memberships of the contributing religions. It's important to add that sensibilities of every faith will be taken into account in these basic services, so that a Buddhist child, for example, will be well fed as appropriately as an elderly Orthodox Jew.

Another of the pyramids will be devoted to a variety of wonderful interfaith healing arts, East meets West, ancient meets high-tech, all faiths contributing their skills and disciplines toward improving the mental and physical health of whoever enters and asks. The Hindus will perform chakra cleansings, let's say. (Chakras are the seven energy centers of the body that correspond to the seven endocrine glands.) A group of Protestant UCLA graduates who studied Dr. Thelma Moss's work with auras and Kirlian photography might specialize in a combination of touch and colored lights that spiral through the body—green for healing, red to help increase and regulate circulation, blue to calm the mind and lower blood pressure, yellow to stimulate spiritual renewal. Buddhists could lead yoga and meditation classes, and on and on and on. One of the many joys of this particular pyramid is that every person of any faith who visits for healing will come to enjoy and respect the benefits of the disciplines of other faiths, and classes will be offered to anyone who wants to learn any of these skills.

The third pyramid will be a magnificent library, still stocked with actual books in 2025, if you can imagine that, as well as state-of-the-art computers, and the only part of the Healing Centers that even vaguely resembles propaganda, although it will be purely factual and not one bit mandatory. The history and principles of each religion participating in the Centers will be brilliantly represented in the library by way of a virtual-reality exhibition, so that the curious can explore and the devout can continually reconnect with their faith.

The fourth pyramid will be multileveled inside, open around a hushed atrium of soft, filtered light, reserved exclusively for prayer, worship, communion, meditation—whatever personal forms of loving expression toward God anyone feels moved to take time for at any hour of the day or night. Each religion represented at the Center will have a designate in attendance at all times for anyone who needs him or her—a priest, for example, for any Catholics who want to make a confession, or a rabbi for any Jews in need of private guidance. But the critical phrase is "for anyone who needs." No one will be turned away by any of the designates, nor will any area of this fourth pyramid or of the Healing Centers around the world be off-limits to anyone. The minute the shadow of discrimination enters the picture at a Healing Center, the whole point will have been lost.

Building Out from the Centers

As the value of the Healing Centers becomes more and more apparent to each participating religion, the communities the Centers call home and the world in general, the generous flood of donations (tax deductible, of course) will make it possible to build, equip and staff a series of structures around the Centers' perimeter that will only increase their already incalculable value.

The Arts Building, for example, will house constantly changing exhibits of paintings, sculpture, music and all other art forms, reflecting religious expression from faiths around the world. Artists passing through will be able to find simple, comfortable lodging in the Arts Building, in exchange for a few hours of teaching or giving lectures on their particular craft in the large domed central studio/lecture hall.

The Research and Ideas Building will be equipped with basic state-of-the-art laboratory facilities and reciprocal computer access to infinite global interfaith research institutes, where great visiting scientific minds from every religion will contribute their ideas to solutions for the earth's most pressing problems, from health issues to pollution to hunger to drought to renewing the ozone layer. A separate annex of the building, its atmosphere designed to embrace its visitors in serenity, reflection and the art of contemplative listening as well as speaking, will be dedicated to a kind of perpetual salon. Priests, rabbis, monks, gurus, prophets—any designate who chooses to, from any and every religion, will be able to gather safely there to discuss ideas, philosophies, goals, hopes and even questions and deeply personal doubts of some kind he or she might not be able to share in any other forum. The only two requirements for entry into this stunningly peaceful annex will be an open mind and a vow of unfailing mutual respect for the sincerity of the beliefs of everyone who enters, whether you entirely agree with the beliefs themselves or not.

The Outreach Building will be the command post for a never-ending battalion of volunteers whose service will be dedicated to the needs of the community around them: meals, medicine and grocery deliveries, letter writing, trips to and from appointments and other simple tasks for those who are unable to manage for themselves; visits to long-term-care hospital patients, particularly children; trained, in-home grief counseling on request for those who've lost loved ones; being a perpetually ready mobilized force on local search parties. Whenever someone within the community, or the community itself, asks for help, out loud or silently, the Outreach Building will be prepared to respond, both on its own and in conjunction with local emergency and law enforcement personnel.

The Dedication School will be possibly the most extraordinary of all the buildings on the perimeter of the Healing Centers. Four stories tall and crescent-shaped, it will provide specialized classes for those who have decided to devote their lives to service in their respective religions. This school will not replace the intensive long-term studies of rabbinical programs, monasteries, convents, and so on. Instead, it will function as a kind of "prep school" for those intensive studies, offering preliminary, broad-based courses in each religion and the general religious and humanitarian responsibilities of rabbis, priests, nuns, ministers, and the like. Courses will be taught by visiting religious teachers from around the world, and of profound interest will be the fact that no one will "graduate" from this one-year school until he or she has completed basic courses in each of the religions taught there. So a person preparing to enter the Protestant ministry, for example, will proceed to long-term schooling with the added perspective of God according to Hinduism, Buddhism,

Catholicism, Judaism, Islam, the Ba'hai faith and various other religions in every corner of the globe, not to mention friends and former classmates who've devoted their lives to every one of those religions. It may be one of the most extraordinary but subtle ways of all in which each religion ends up being of the greatest benefit to its membership, thanks to the contributions of all, without for a moment compromising its own beliefs.

On a personal note: I consider myself a Gnostic Christian, utterly devoted to God, and Christ as the Son of God, with Mary as His Blessed Mother, but not devoted to the rules or dogma of any denomination as being "the only right way." In fact, in my home you'll find a Buddha, the Bible, the Koran, the Torah, a magnificent painting of Jesus, Angels everywhere, a miniature Hindu elephant statue and on, and on, and on. My adoration of God is not dependent on what name He's called by, and I can't imagine bearing anything but gratitude and awe in my heart for any of the messengers He sent to light the eternal path between Him and us. So when I say I believe that someday all religions will come together for the benefit of all other religions, because we all have knowledge and answers that can supplement without negating one another, I want you to know how deeply and currently I'm living that belief.

I'm also excited by my certainty that there will be another source of divine inspiration behind the Healing Centers who will be openly recognized by all the religions that collaborate to make them happen. And it's about time—She will have been waiting almost three thousand years by then for a renewal of the mainstream acknowledgment of Her rightful place beside God, our Father.

Azna, the Mother God

Azna and God are not an "either/or" concept, not a radical choice between a male or female God, or some jarring adjustment to be made in your belief system, but simply a more expansive perspective on our Creator that was accepted and celebrated even before the time of Christ.

The Mother God is the emotional, nurturing aspect of the deity, just as the Father

God is the logical, intellectual aspect. She gives us our hope and serenity while He gives us our strength and our indomitable courage. Together, They are the Godhead, each complete and each omnipotent, loving us beyond all judgments and conditions. That the Father God would unite the religions, and that the Mother God would lend the purpose of healing, is only one of a universe of testaments to their complementary Perfection.

In the early 2020s, even before the Healing Centers officially take shape, open celebrations of Azna will begin taking place worldwide, with a global interfaith Feast Day of Peace in Her honor. On that day, even in the most terroristic and obscene of wars, out of some combination of reverence, respect or cowardly superstition among those who don't know Her that they'll incur Her wrath, not a single gun will be drawn or a single shot fired.

Throughout this book, to this point and from now on, you'll notice that I exclusively use singular masculine pronouns like He and Him to refer to God. That has nothing to do with disregard for Azna, and it's not something my publisher has insisted on. It's a purely practical choice on my part—I'm guessing that you'd find constant references to God as He/She and Him/Her as irritating to read as it would be for me to write. Mother God understands. I hope you will too.

The Center of the Centers

At the heart of each of the Healing Centers will be a most exquisite oblong building, made of glass, surrounded by quiet waterfalls, groves of tall trees, stone pathways and, sadly but necessarily, very discreet but brilliant security systems and guards.

This building will be simply but beautifully appointed, filled with candles and comfort and dignity and privacy. There will be a common dining room, sitting room and library, with an adjacent kitchen attended by chefs from the appropriate participating religions. Surrounding the common rooms will be private quarters, all of equal size, lovely but not luxurious.

The private quarters will be reserved for any visiting dignitaries of the religions who contribute to the Healing Centers, any of whom might find themselves sitting down to dinner together or enjoying a cup of tea in the library together. Examples today might be the Dalai Lama, Pope John Paul II and Billy Graham all lodging one night in the safe, private sanctity of the Center in Geneva, let's say, and sharing a meal around the same table before they retire for the evening—no aides, no entourages, no media, just three devout men, their interpreters and their common lifelong devotion to God and humankind.

Healing Centers will become valuable sources of local pride, comfort, hope, faith and unity in the areas where they're located. They'll also become homes away from home for the traveling devoted, searching and sought after. It will become as common to ask about the location of the Healing Center nearest to a destination we're about to visit as it will be to ask about hotels and tourist attractions, and communities around the world will combine resources to bring new Healing Centers closer to their own neighborhoods.

It seems like a shame that we have to wait until 2025 for Healing Centers to come along, doesn't it, when so many of us could use them *today*?

The Antichrist

There's been a lot of talk about the coming Antichrist, including in this book, especially in the Nostradamus pages. Some believe the prophecy of the Antichrist has been fulfilled in the persona of Saddam Hussein. Others believe the Antichrist's name on this earth is Osama bin Laden.

I have my own prophecy about the Antichrist, and I guess this chapter is as appropriate a place as any to discuss it.

I do believe we need to brace ourselves for an Antichrist, but I don't believe he's arrived yet. He'll be born in 2005 or 2006, in the area of Syria. It will be in about 2030 that he makes his proclamation that he is the resurrected Christ, back for the Rapture, and that all those who follow him will be saved.

He will have long, jet black hair to his shoulders, and huge brown eyes. Unlike Saddam Hussein and Osama bin Laden, his seduction will begin with great pretense of compassion, nonviolence and a desire for world peace and unity. He'll have a charismatic gift and a feigned humility that sends him at the beginning of his "ministry" to gather his first followers from among the poor, who are easily and cheaply bribed for the smallest amount of food and sense of hope. He himself will live in caves and tents while his reputation takes hold, gathering donations for his followers, none of which he appears to be spending on himself but all of which it will be revealed later he's hoarding and investing to amass a fortune. He will have a genius for manipulation and be a master mentalist, psychologist and self-promoter.

His soft-spoken "pacifism," "humanitarianism" and undeniable charisma will attract a celebrity following, first in Europe and then in the United States, generating still more "donations." By the time his rhetoric begins to turn slowly and shrewdly genocidal and his vast holdings include black market nuclear weapons, he'll have a slavish, indebted and systematically indoctrinated flock of converts numbering in the hundreds of thousands, ready to kill for him and die for him in the tragic belief that he's their only path to eternal salvation.

If you can block their respective physical images from your mind, a vague parallel from recent history would be the discovery that the Maharishi Mahesh Yogi, say, the soft-spoken, pacifistic celebrity guru of the 1960s—who never claimed to be the reincarnated Christ, I hasten to add—was, in reality, the real brains and money behind al Quaida. It seems ludicrous to even write that or say it out loud, but when this other man "goes public" in around 2030 and then reveals himself to be genuinely and completely evil a few years later, the shock and sense of betrayal will be that jarring and that seemingly impossible.

It's no coincidence that his rise to power will be preceded by Healing Centers and other major and minor collaborative efforts among world religions. It takes great concentrations of Light to eliminate that much insidious, cancerous darkness, whether the Antichrist or just another horrifying terrorist with a different angle, and when bright Light gathers together, no amount of darkness can overcome it.

That's not a prophecy, it's a fact.

It will be a fact in 2030.

It's a fact today.

It's not always as easy to believe as we'd like in these rough, uneasy times, when it looks as if darkness is having its high old despicable way.

But it's still a fact.

We just have to keep our own Lights on "high beam," seek out the other Lights around us, pray for even more Light than ever from the Father and Mother God and ride this out together.

CHAPTER NINE

✳

Education

I was a teacher for eighteen years, so I have mixed feelings about what I see as the distant future of education. On one hand, I wish there were a way to take our current system and make it work so that every child could go to a safe, decent, reasonably sized classroom and be stimulated enough about learning at his or her own level of ability to look forward to school. On the other hand—yeah, right.

What lies ahead is geared toward our children's safety and protection from violence, drugs, a lazy and/or overwhelmed and/or underpaid faculty and too much rhetoric about the importance of education while school budgets continue to be an embarrassment. As if I'm telling you anything you don't already know far too well if you have children or simply watch the news every once in a while.

The massive changes in the whole structure of the education system will take place around 2020. They'll make complete sense by then, to the point where we'll look back on where we are now and wonder how we ever got through it with as many of our children educated and intact as they are.

The Grade School Years

The early years of a child's education, preschool through sixth grade, are going to be extraordinary. There will be no more than ten or fifteen students in any given classroom, and teachers will be well paid and highly qualified. No teacher will even be allowed into the school system, in fact, without an added degree in child psychology and a *thorough* background check. The same will be true of every teacher's assistant, whose responsibilities will include special attention to children who seem to be having trouble in certain subjects or even trouble with other classmates or at home. Children's educational and emotional needs will be considered of equal importance during these early years, and when either of those needs isn't being met, a team of tutors, counselors and neurologically trained psychiatrists will be on call.

In addition to the usual basic subjects of reading, writing, math, social studies, spelling, and so on, grade school students will also take classes in nutrition, basic ethics, one art course of their choice and at least one foreign language of their choice. Parents or guardians will be held accountable for chronically incomplete homework assignments, absences and tardiness, and attendance by at least one parent at bimonthly parent-teacher meetings will be mandatory. The "or else" will be heavy fines, payable to the state, with the funds being used strictly for the education system, or parenting classes three times a week until the parent's encouragement and support of his or her child's formative school years is clearly established. The attitude that "it's my business how I raise my child" will be viewed as simply idiotic, since the truth is that on many levels we deal every day with the adult versions of how someone raised a child, and it's not always a pretty sight.

In order for grade school administrators to keep their jobs, which by then will be very desirable, lucrative positions, and avoid being replaced by a long line of eager and highly qualified applicants, the following mandates will be enforced:

* No child will graduate from the sixth grade without knowing how to read and write.
* No child will graduate from the sixth grade without being in the habit of learning and succeeding and completing assignments on time.
* No child will graduate from the sixth grade without thinking of school as a safe place of positive individual attention based on his or her own abilities.
* And no child will graduate from the sixth grade without knowing that the adult or adults in charge of him or her at home think the child's education is so important that they're actually willing to participate in it instead of just

lecturing the child about it and then strolling off to watch TV for the rest of the evening.

I know. This all sounds like Fantasy Land, where we'll get the money for all this from a great big hundred-dollar-bill tree in that hundred-dollar-bill orchard we all have in our backyards. And we'll get all those added classrooms from the Tooth Fairy, right?

Not quite. By around 2020 we're going to get the money for all that, and all those added classrooms, from middle schools and high schools, which are going to save a fortune in overhead and leave a whole lot of school buildings vacant for the grade schoolers to scale down to their modest little heights and take over.

Middle School and High School

As I said, by the time a child leaves sixth grade, it will be imperative for him or her to have well-established study habits, and for parents to be well-trained watchdogs about those study habits. Because in 2020, instead of classrooms, teachers will teach from several different education centers throughout each state, via computer.

Every student will have a laptop-like link to their assigned teachers at the student's assigned education center, and those teachers will have an easily accessed "roll" grid to make it instantly apparent who's signed on and who's absent. In fact, truancy will be more glaringly conspicuous than it is now, showing up as it will at the end of each day on a computer printout, and local authorities will be dispatched so quickly that both truants and parents will find it much more convenient for the child to just return to his or her laptop/school after all.

Not only will the students receive a hologram image of their teachers and teaching aides through these computers, but the teachers can access any of their students with a single keyboard stroke as well. So opening your laptop and then heading off to the movies will be a useless exercise and be marked as truancy. But this will also allow the experience to be interactive between teachers and students, so that if a student is having trouble with something, the teacher can actually see it and talk the student through it instead of just responding to it with a series of "instant messages." All computers in each classroom—the teacher's and the students'—will be interconnected, so that class discussions can take place on-screen and often with considerably less self-consciousness than in a "live" setting, in which the simple act of raising your hand to speak can be daunting for the shy or more naturally reserved students.

Homework is submitted and graded by computer, obviously, except for term papers, book reports and other written assignments. Those are graded by graduate students in the teaching curriculum as an essential part of *their* homework assignments, so any danger of subjective grading or teacher overload is eliminated.

Tests in each subject will be given every three months, local, live and in person, on a Saturday, in the same buildings used as grade schools during the week. Based on test scores, students in need of extra help and remedial work will attend small tutored classes in those same buildings, scheduled to not interfere with grade school hours, until their grades improve.

In addition to traditional middle school and high school subjects, students will also be required to continue with a minimum number of hours in a foreign language, nutrition and ethics.

Physical Education

Three hours of physical education per week, at those same grade school facilities, will be required for all middle school and high school students. Physical education instructors will teach those courses exclusively, will have to be trained in both Eastern and Western sports and movement disciplines and will be required to have degrees in basic physical therapy and sports injuries.

Each student will be given a thorough physical examination at regular intervals during the school year, by a qualified medical professional, at the school's expense. Based on the results of those exams, a variety of programs will be designed, so that every student will be challenged but no student will be pushed beyond his or her safe physical capacity.

Students will also be offered enough options, and enough opportunities to change preferences, that they'll be encouraged to find some form of activity they can enjoy. In addition to the usual track, gymnastics, aerobics, basketball, soccer and other traditionally strenuous physical education activities, such choices as yoga, fencing, karate, aikido and tae kwon do will be available.

Trying your best will warrant top grades in physical education. Repeatedly not trying will warrant a failing grade, as will disrespect toward any fellow student who's making an honest effort at whatever activity he or she has chosen.

Special Aptitudes

Even now, thanks to the magic of computers, we can send an infinite array of sounds and images from one corner of the world to another. By 2020, today's computer's will probably look as archaic as the twelve-inch black-and-white TV with rabbit ears my family sat glued to in the 1950s, which I was sure technology couldn't possibly top in my lifetime.

Just as there were when I was teaching, there will be students in 2020 who will be so gifted at some art or science or skill that, even from the relative distance of the education centers, teachers can't help but sit up and take notice.

Unlike when I was teaching, though, teachers will now be able to do something significant about it.

Students' artwork, science reports, dance or music performances, mechanical designs, and so on, will be able to be sent to special schools all over the country, or all over the globe for that matter. So without ever changing locations or missing a beat in their other studies, gifted high school artists will be able to take classes at the Sorbonne in Paris, or budding geniuses in mechanical engineering who happen to be average eighth graders in every other way can begin some preliminary courses at MIT.

Extracurricular Activities

Students will still be able to try out for sports teams, school bands, clubs and any other extracurricular activities they choose to vent their "socializing steam," using the grade school facilities after hours.

There will just be a couple of added conditions to participating in these activities, both of which must be agreed to in writing by the student's parent or guardian prior to trying out: No students may participate in any extracurricular school activity unless they maintain a B average or higher; and every student participating in any extracurricular school activity will submit to random drug testing. Failing a drug test will result in an immediate thirty-day suspension, which the student will spend in an in-house drug rehabilitation facility at his or her parents' expense, with all appropriate involvement of local law enforcement.

All students' extracurricular activity reports, like reports on their performance in physical education, will be sent to their respective education centers to be entered into their increasingly detailed computer file.

Higher Education

In addition to students being able to apply to colleges and universities around the world via computer, colleges and universities around the world will now have a vast, ready global databank, through access to each of the education centers, from which to recruit students in whom they might be interested, scholastically or athletically. Oxford University in England could easily offer a scholarship to a uniquely gifted young scholar without knowing (or ultimately caring) that this gifted young scholar is from a small town in Kansas with a population of less than two hundred people. Or thanks to a simple computer "search" engine, colleges from Australia to Europe to South America could get into a bidding war for some talented soccer player in upstate New York, provided the student keeps his or her grades up and stays drug free throughout junior high and high school.

Of course, if students, colleges and universities around the world are this sophisticated and connected in cyberspace, you can bet potential employers, professional sports teams and "scouts" in every area of the arts will be every bit as wide awake and tuned in. International recruiting, "headhunting" and mining for artistic talent will in itself become one of the hottest, most competitive careers on the map.

And a personal aside, only an opinion for the present and future, that I just want to get off my chest as a former teacher and a current adoring grandmother: if any child goes from junior high into high school without being able to name one activity or subject they're really good at, that they also happen to really enjoy, we've done that child a terrible disservice.

There. So. At any rate, as I said when this chapter began, I have mixed feelings about the 2020 picture of education centers, and students being so separate from their teachers and one another during class time, and the hands-on approach to teaching becoming yet another yellowing page in the history of "progress."

But about an education system that actually educates? And reallocates its money in such a way that teachers are well qualified and well paid, and the bulk of the personal attention goes to grade school children, who need it most? And doesn't just hope for but demands parental involvement in children's education? And gives children opportunities for extended and higher education they might never have a prayer of getting today? And takes meaningful action against drugs and even disrespect? And, please, God, maybe prevents there ever again being one more Columbine implosion?

I guess my feelings about this aren't quite as mixed as I thought they were.

CHAPTER TEN

✳

Technology

Let me tell you about my expertise in the world of technology. I was recently given a gorgeous TV from a very generous organization I've worked with for several years. (I'd love to name them and give credit where it's due, but their modesty prevails.) I love this TV. It's one of those huge flat-panel screens you can hang on the wall like a painting if you want, as state-of-the-art as it gets, and I immediately had it installed in my bedroom, where I'd see it most often when I'm at home. There's just one small problem with my beautiful new TV: I can't figure out for the life of me how to turn the damned thing on and off, or how to change channels. I've spent more time studying the remote control than I spent with one of my ex-husbands, and I still end up having to yell for my assistant, Ben, who doesn't even ask what I want anymore when he hears me call his name. He just walks in, gently takes the remote from me, turns on the TV, finds whatever channel he knows I'll want, pats me sympathetically on the shoulder and leaves the room again, all without saying a word.

I'm really a very bright woman, and I accept that like everyone else, I'm simply better at some things than I am at others. Technology is one of those "others." I appreciate the benefits of technology more than I can say. In fact, I'm crazy about some of them. I don't have to look back too many years to remember a much less convenient life without my cell phone and my website, for example, both of which make me instantly accessible from any corner of this planet. They amaze me. Do I have a clue how or why they work? No. Do I care? No. But not a day goes by when I don't appreciate them.

All of which is simply to point out that when I'm given prophetic information on technology, no matter how brilliant and intricate it might be, it's still being filtered through the mind I've just described to you. And then I pass the information on to Lindsay, my coauthor and friend, who'll never be confused with an MIT graduate either. So if the prophecies in this chapter aren't always as precise or detailed as some of you might wish they were, or if they're limited in their scope—all I can tell you is, you're getting everything I've got in the best way Lindsay and I know to describe it. We promise to stop short of using nonsense words like "thingy" and "doodad."

The Future at Home

New houses by about 2015 will be both solar-powered and prefabricated. "Prefab" in 2015 won't have the same "cardboard box" connotation it sometimes has today. These prefabricated houses will be as modest or as exquisite as their owners can afford, just like now, but made of materials that have to adhere to far stricter safety codes than we can dream of, usually stone or flame-retardant synthetic wood over reinforced steel, with roofs of ceramic tile and solar panels that will neither shatter nor burn no matter what the natural or human-made disaster.

Sophisticated security systems will be as common in every home as doors and windows. At first that seems odd, since crime rates are down by 2015. But it makes sense when you realize that crime rates are down partly *because* sophisticated home security systems start becoming common in about 2011. Even the most ornately hand-carved wooden doors are filled with reinforced steel, much like the exterior walls. The windows are unbreakable glass, able to be opened only by the homeowner, by another approved person or by the home's central computer, in an emergency when the fire alarm goes off, for example.

Doors and windows will no longer have visible, traditional locks that can be picked or tampered with. Instead, the security system allows access inside not by a numerical code or password, but by "eyeprints." There will be peepholes at all access points to the house, and placing your eye on or near the peephole will allow the computer to scan the configuration of the cornea and iris. Like fingerprints and DNA, each person's cornea and iris configuration is distinctive, and the configuration of everyone who's authorized to enter the house will be on file in the computer.

If an unauthorized person is foolish enough to try to force entry into the house, by the way, both the security company and the police will be alerted and immediately dispatched. In the meantime, the home security computer, which will have already recorded every move of the would-be intruder on its hard drive, will activate a boundary of lasers or impenetrable electrical charges of some kind around the perimeter of the property that will detain this person until the authorities arrive.

When an authorized person, let's say the homeowner, does gain entry to the house, though, the steel-core door will unlock and open, lights will come on and the security computer will scan the interior of the house and confirm that all is well and everything's safe. That same computer will then perform a series of tasks that are predetermined by the homeowner, who controls the computer by simply speaking commands into it. Music plays, TV comes on throughout the house, the oven starts, the hot tub begins bubbling—whatever you've asked your arrival to trigger will spring into action without your having to push a single button or even give it a thought.

By the way, here's something I'd run out and buy today if it were available: showers will have as many jets as we want, just like they do now, but when you've finished your shower, you'll simply stay right where you are and be flash-dried by some combination of heat, lights and thermal energy. Including your hair. In ten seconds or less. I'd like one of those in every color, please.

And then there's the phone system. In addition to wireless headsets when you want privacy, the voice-activated system will be set up through that same computer, with virtually invisible microphones and speakers throughout the house—or, to put it another way, I have no idea where they are or how this happens, I just wish I had it now. But as you go about your business once you're home, you'll simply say the word "Messages," and your messages will be played back for you over these centralized speakers. Many of them may have been taken care of, and calls may have been made, by the computer per your instructions before you left. Let's say you're expecting a call from Mary to set up a meeting on Friday, and you're only available until 11:00. You also need Smith & Jones Plumbing to come on Tuesday to repair a leak, and you can be home anytime after noon. Through these central speakers, while you go right on with what you're doing, you'll hear the computer's conversation with Mary and its call to Smith & Jones Plumbing.

Automatic dialing will be stored in the computer, of course, so that you can simply say, "Call Lindsay" while you're putting away your groceries or feeding the dogs, and the computer will call all the numbers it has for her in the order of where it's most likely to find her. Conference calling will have expanded into its truest meaning by then as well, so that you could also say, "Chris and Paul and I need to talk to Pam, Hillary, Fern, Beth and Walter," and within moments all of you who are available will be on the phone together no matter where in the world you all happen to be.

I know. You're wondering about video phones. And yes, this same central phone system will have available cameras and projectors as well, so anyone and everyone you're talking to will be displayed on monitors throughout the house. I'm not especially sold on the idea of video phones myself—I don't necessarily care to be presentable every time I talk on the phone, and I like knowing I can make faces if I want to, or pretend to be listening intently while actually refilling my saltshakers. But by 2015 when all of this is in full fruition, video phones will have been perfected and almost everyone but me will have one.

Crank calls, threatening calls and harassing calls can be both recorded by this same home computer and traced with the push of a button, so that you'll be able to hand the police recordings of the calls themselves and proof of the numbers they originated from.

Telemarketers will have long since vanished by 2015. What laws don't accomplish toward wiping them out, public awareness will—people will simply stop doing any business with them at all, and you can count on it that when profits vanish, so will the telemarketers.

Another of my favorite features of this phone system is that with the same voice commands, you can tell it, "No calls," and you won't even hear your phone ring. Or you can say, "No calls except from the office," and your phone will only ring and the call will only be connected if the computer recognizes the number or voice of someone from your office.

And the ever-vigilant voice-activated computer will always be on nonstop security alert, so that your simply yelling, "Police!" or "Fire!" or "Ambulance!" or even "Help!" will trigger all the appropriate calls. Emergency vehicles will be on their way in less time than it takes us right now to get to the phone and dial 9-1-1, and it doesn't take a prophet to foresee that the number of tragedies averted and lives saved by that one feature alone will be impossible to calculate.

It's no big surprise that personal robots will be available by 2015. How many decades have inventors been trying to come up with them now? By 2015 they'll be a fixture in most upscale homes, and they'll be more affordable to the general public by

2019. In the beginning of their daily in-home use they'll be convenience items, able on voice command to cook, clean, serve drinks and meals, make beds, put away laundry and feed pets. They'll be the result of wonderful collaborations between technologists and artists, designed for maximum movement and efficiency but also given a wide variety of physical characteristics, either off the assembly line or custom made to the buyer's preference, so that they'll quickly feel less like machines and more like "live" parts of the household, with names and even preprogrammed résumés and bios if the buyer chooses.

As the use of robots becomes more widespread and reasonably priced, their potential usefulness will continue to grow by leaps and bounds as well. By 2019, when robots are capable of responding to between five and six hundred complicated voice commands, they'll be brilliant "watchdogs" for infants in the house, for example. They will be able to spend the night in the nursery, gently turning the baby over at specified time intervals as a safeguard against SIDS, or respond instantly if the baby is in any danger of getting caught in the rungs of the crib. With older children, robots will be able to read stories, recite literature and poetry, help with homework and teach such basics as the alphabet and beginning computer skills.

For those of you who are concerned that some parents will start letting robots take on responsibilities that the parents themselves should be in charge of, don't worry—they will. Sadly, it's a guarantee. But look at it this way. For single working parents, robots will be a Godsend and a well-deserved helping hand. As for lazy, disinterested parents, they would have shifted the responsibility somewhere else anyway, or neglected it entirely, so at least their children will have someone/something by their side to pay attention instead of no one/nothing at all.

Technology at Random

Think of the last time you saw a slide show—those of you who are old enough to remember what slide shows are—and you'll have some idea of how I received these images in my mind. If some of them sound suspiciously inspired by James Bond movies, let me assure you, any resemblance is completely coincidental. I've seen maybe two James Bond movies in my life, and all I got out of them was a giant crush on Sean Connery, just like every other woman I know.

* By 2007 cell phones will be as capable as current corded phones of extensive video conferencing with widespread groups of people.
* Wireless TVs as tiny as cell phones will be available by 2010. They'll be able to tap into any satellite signal with perfect reception, and their picture can either be viewed on the tiny screen or projected onto any available flat surface and magnified to any convenient size with no significant loss of quality.
* In 2008 wristwatches will hit the market that, in addition to all the bells and whistles of today's watches, will also record conversations and take and send digital photographs. Like cell phones, the early models of these wristwatches will be popular but cum-

bersome compared to the small, elegant, streamlined versions that will come along just a few short years later.

✳ In around 2012 there will be eyeglasses and/or sunglasses that will also double as digital recorders, cameras and transmitters, as well as personal stereo systems, kind of the boombox or Walkman in designer sunglass form. An extension on one stem of the glasses will act as an earpiece to prevent public places from becoming the nightmarish insanity of countless songs all playing at once.

✳ Building codes for every home, store and other public building by 2013 will include a mandate for silent, powerful, well-concealed air purifiers, so that airborne viruses will be virtually eliminated and all sources of asthma attacks and allergies will be filtered out of the air before they can do any harm. Aromatherapy will be advanced and refined enough by then that as the air is filtered and purified, it will also be treated with very subtle, almost imperceptible health-building essences.

✳ By 2040 most private homes will be three stories high, with retractable roofs to allow the family hovercraft to come and go.

Other technological advances are mentioned throughout this book, obviously, in areas ranging from medicine to ecology and topography to forensics. And even so I haven't begun to scratch the surface of everything we have to look forward to, any more than I believe that someone in 1900 could have predicted every breakthrough of the last century, from the telephone to the computer to the space shuttle to cloning.

One thing I want to mention here, though, that I think could be a step in the right direction if it's handled wisely and fairly is that innovators around the world, in a wide variety of areas, are going to start getting some real incentives and rewards for their hard work. About ten years from now, panels of experts will be chosen by their peers to accept submissions of innovations and breakthroughs in their respective fields. These experts will be authorized to secure funding for the pursuit and expansion of those breakthroughs, and to publish the names of those responsible. If they happen to be Americans, the federal and state governments, through some kind of point system, will reward these inventors and innovators with significant tax deductions.

Again, the areas in which the people behind these innovations will be rewarded will be widely varied enough to include all sorts of talents and all sorts of income brackets, so that we'll finally show signs of having our priorities straight. Education, the arts, medicine, forensic science, architecture, horticulture, psychiatry, veterinary medicine, textiles, geology—any innovation in any field that could ultimately benefit humankind will be treated with equal regard, equal funding and equal tax benefits for those we have to thank for them.

Believe me, no one's more in favor than I am of being careful never to take life so seriously that we lose our ability to escape and have a good laugh, especially at ourselves. But wouldn't it be great if, thanks to an equal celebration of all contributions to society, as many people could name the three men who discovered DNA as can name the cast of the most recent season of *Survivor*?

(By the way, James Watson, Francis Crick and Maurice Wilson shared the Nobel Prize in 1962 for discovering the structure of DNA.)

CHAPTER ELEVEN

✳

Crime Fighting and Forensics

Some of the prophecies in this book will be controversial. Here's one that won't: we'll never see a day when crime ceases to exist. I wish that weren't true. I really wish I could get a quick glimpse of a day on this earth when there'll be no more greed, no more cruel inhumanity, no more of that amoral sense of entitlement that lies at the heart of deliberate criminal behavior. But since I can't, and since we're all stuck dealing with facts, not wishes, we have to look elsewhere for hope about our future safety and protection. And the good news is, we can find that hope in the brilliant advancements that lie ahead in the worlds of law enforcement and the science of crime-solving known as forensics.

Those of you who follow my career are aware of my decades of involvement with local, state and federal police agencies across the continent. I don't charge a dime for this work, and I never, ever solicit it. I'm not an "ambulance chaser." In fact, I think it's obscene to barge in on someone's tragedy uninvited, especially if there's the glimmer of a spotlight involved. If I get a "hit" on an unsolved case I've heard about, I'll discreetly contact the authorities in charge and give them the information to do with as they please. But beyond that, if I'm not asked, I stay out of it.

And above all, I keep my mouth shut. For one thing, some of the cases I've worked on are dangerous, and I'm not about to expose my family and friends to possible retribution from someone I've helped put away. For another thing, I'm a realist. I know that a psychic showing up in the midst of a criminal investigation can create a flurry of tabloid headlines, compromise the credibility of the investigation depending on that particular psychic's motives and track record and, worst of all, wrongly divert the focus of the case. Suddenly the spotlight shifts to whether or not psychics are legitimate, or how desperate the police or the family must be to have called one in, or what gossip everyone can dredge up from the psychic's past (plenty in my case, and I'll save them the effort and dredge it up myself for the world to see). And in the midst of all that noise, the victim(s), the agony their loved ones are going through and the search for whoever's responsible get drowned out, when the fact is, nothing else really matters.

Very early one morning, long before dawn, my cell phone woke me out of a sound sleep. It was my assistant, his voice quiet but urgent.

"Sorry, Sylvia, but I need to put through a call that came into the office. Trust me, you want to take this one."

I muttered something incoherent during a couple of clicks. Then I heard a woman on the line. She was polite, soft-spoken and, looking back, as inspiring an example of grace under fire as I've ever come across.

"Ms. Browne," she said, "please forgive me, I never meant for you to be awakened at this hour, I was simply going to leave a message."

I managed a vague pronunciation of "Who is this?"

She told me, and in an instant I was wide awake. I'll call her Mrs. Q. Sadly, as everyone in the country was aware, Mrs. Q.'s daughter had been murdered. This brutal murder and the ongoing search for the killer were making national headlines, Mrs. Q. and her husband were in the throes of anguish the rest of us can only begin to imagine, and she was worried about my losing a couple hours' sleep?

"I'm so glad you called," I assured her, praying she could hear how much I meant it. "What can I do for you? Anything. Name it, what can I do, how can I help?"

As it turned out, she'd read some of my books and seen several of my TV appearances, and she trusted me at a time in her life when trust was a rare commodity. She was reaching out to me for any psychic insight I might lend to the investigation, but she was also reaching out for comfort, support and a whole lot of spiritual reassurance. I was touched, I was honored and I was ready to go wherever she wanted me to be whenever she needed me there if we could just figure out how to discreetly make that happen.

Incredibly, we couldn't. Even though by sheer coincidence we were less than an hour's drive from each other at the time, the press was camped out around the clock at every entrance to her house, and rabid reporters followed her and her husband everywhere they went. One glimpse of me anywhere near either of them or the family home and all of us, including the police, would have been confronted with headlines reading "Psychic Joins Hunt for Killer," adding nothing but more turmoil to an already unbearable situation.

So instead, there we sat, Mrs. Q. and I, in the predawn darkness, on opposite ends of the phone, this sweet, brave, decimated woman who desperately needed a hug and me wanting just as desperately to give her one and hating that I couldn't—not because I was unavailable or too far away, but because, as a recognized psychic, my presence in the midst of a murder story that had captured the nation's rapt attention would only have added to the sideshow.

*   *   *

The good news—and I swear it's good news, no matter how much the close-minded skeptics out there will scoff and sneer about it—is that by around 2010, law enforcement's use of psychics will come "out of the closet" and be a commonplace, widely accepted collaboration, as opposed to its current status as something only a handful of detectives, police officers and federal agents are brave enough and honest enough to own up to.

The key will be a kind of "registry" of psychics and other paranormal specialists to whom law enforcement agencies will turn as routinely as they now turn to criminal profilers, forensic sketch artists and sculptors, blood spatter experts and other gifted human resources who've proven themselves to be invaluable investigative tools despite a whole lot of early ill-informed cynicism about their credibility. No individuals will be listed on this registry who haven't earned their way there, by their track records in the field of crime solving, by exhaustive objective testing and by thorough screening and background checks. Frauds, convicted felons, mentalist lounge acts with hidden microphones, publicity-hungry scam artists and unemployed psychic hotline operators need not apply. The registry will also be updated and reviewed on a regular basis, to make sure that all the paranormal specialists listed are continuing to do their share for the law enforcement community, that they're maintaining an admirable reputation and that they're not compromising their discretion in any way, for any amount of money, under any circumstance.

In other words, in about 2010, I'll be able to push through a horde of media and walk right up to Mrs. Q.'s door without seeming any more noteworthy to the press than criminal profiler Robert Ressler, the amazing forensic artist Jeanne Boylan or any of the other specialists who are routinely called in on major investigations.

Until then, Mrs. Q., just so you know, even though time has passed and you've done a wonderful job of getting on with your life with your usual courage and grace, I haven't forgotten that I still owe you that hug. As for the man who killed your daughter, by the way, I'll word this carefully to keep myself and Dutton out of any legal trouble: he's been correctly identified, and he'll get exactly what's coming to him.

DNA

The discovery of DNA, the genetic blue-print that makes every person on earth unique (with the exception of identical twins, whose DNA is as identical as they are), was without a doubt one of the most significant contributions to humankind in the twentieth century. DNA has impacted our society in countless ways, but one of the most valuable and highly publicized, of course, is in the area of criminal investigation.

We all know about the crimes that have been solved beyond a reasonable doubt thanks to DNA, the prisoners who've been set free when DNA proved they'd been wrongly convicted, and the bodies that might never have been identified if DNA hadn't been available. We also know that the legal system and civil libertarians concerned with our individual rights to privacy and protection against self-incrimination have fought hard to protect those who don't want to voluntarily offer a DNA sample. At the same time there are those who believe that the interest of public safety can best be served by more widespread DNA sampling and easier access to those results. It's a difficult, passionate debate, with valid points being made on both sides.

What lies ahead isn't likely to calm things down for the first few years, but once it's under way the benefits to law enforcement and the safety and welfare of the general public will be undeniable.

Many state and national DNA databases already exist. As early as 1990 the FBI instituted a program called CODIS (which stands for Combined DNA Index System), which makes it possible for local, state and national forensic labs to record and compare DNA profiles with the huge federal index of criminal offenders' DNA on file in the CODIS computers. A "hit" on any of these databases can instantly and positively identify a criminal or link a series of crimes that might have appeared to be unrelated. But obviously a "hit" can't happen if the offender's DNA hasn't been entered into those databases. And murder victims found with no identification can remain unidentified for an agonizing period of time unless they happen to be on file in CODIS or can be traced to a possible relative for DNA

comparison. Not to mention victims of am-
nesia and Alzheimer's disease who are lost
and unable to identify themselves, or ab-
ducted or abandoned children either too
young or too frightened to tell the authorities who they are and where they live, none
of whom are likely to be in any current national DNA database.

I don't want to give the mistaken impression that the United States has cornered
the market on national DNA databases, by
the way. Almost four hundred countries
throughout the world, from England to
Japan to Canada to Iceland to Switzerland
to all of Eastern Europe, have similar computerized indexes, all capable of virtually instantaneous global interaction with one another when it comes to law enforcement.
More countries are either developing databases or considering the possibility. And in
virtually all of these countries the pros and
cons of DNA databases are as passionately
debated as they are here in America.

By around 2010, controversial as it will be
at first, it will be mandated that a DNA sample of every infant born in the United States
is taken and recorded at the time of the
baby's birth. That DNA "fingerprint" will ac-

company every piece of identification created for that individual from then on. School
and hospital records, Social Security card,
driver's license, professional licenses, credit
and bank cards, and so on will all be imprinted with the singular DNA code that's
that individual's and that individual's alone,
and technology by then will be able to scan
it as easily as a bar code. The United States
won't be the first country to implement the
routine DNA sampling of newborn infants,
and we'll be far from the last. It will be a
common worldwide practice within ten
years of its inception.

Even before 2010 local and state governments in America will initiate a program to
encourage the general population to voluntarily have their DNA recorded and linked to
their personal identification. For obvious
reasons, a fair percentage of the population
will politely decline. But a larger percentage
will participate, as will the populations of
other countries. Fortunately, the need for
reliable DNA labs will be met by around
2007, eliminating the backlog of samples
waiting to be tested today, and the result of
this ongoing voluntary DNA testing and the
testing of newborns will be a massive inter-

national database called SCAN. (That acronym came from my Spirit Guide Francine. If she knows what those letters stand for, she's either keeping it to herself or I'm not hearing her.)

SCAN will be perpetually interactive with CODIS and every other law enforcement DNA database around the world, and the results will be overwhelmingly positive. Identity theft and fake IDs will become almost more trouble to accomplish than they're worth, and identifying anonymous murder victims, which once took weeks, months or years, will now take hours at most. Lost, missing, abandoned, and stolen children found on the streets or in the hands of criminals will be able to be reunited with their families within minutes. And any crime scene at which even a first-time offender has left DNA behind will be solved as easily as if the offender had dropped a driver's license and a signed confession on the way out the door.

The international SCAN DNA database will be an essential, invaluable security device for society in general and a staple of law enforcement forensics by 2015. But it's only one of several databases that will work hand in hand to, as so many police departments promise and most live up to, protect and serve.

Database Breakthroughs

Fingerprint databases are already commonplace in the war on crime. The largest and most centralized in the United States is AFIS, the Automated Fingerprint Identification System, where literally tens of millions of prints are stored and accessible to law enforcement for comparison to latent fingerprints found at both current and "cold" crime scenes waiting to be solved. It doesn't take a psychic to predict that the speed and precision of AFIS and smaller, more localized databases will make even today's amazing technology seem obsolete in a matter of just a couple of years. While current databases can bring up prints with a number of similarities to the fingerprint in question, for ultimate comparison by forensic experts studying the prints side by side, databases in the very near future will be able to identify exact matches of entire fingerprints within moments if any exist on file, saving countless hours of those experts' valuable time.

Handprints, footprints and prints of the palm/side of the hand are also being recorded in databases today. The uniqueness of palm/side of the hand prints is a fairly recent awareness that the forensic community is taking brilliant advantage of, and their source is so obvious if you think about it. When we write, we rest the side of the hand we're writing with on the surface we're writing on. Unless we're wearing gloves or writing on something smaller than the length of our hand, it would be almost impossible not to leave a trace of a side-handprint near what we've written, when we could easily leave no fingerprint at all. The fact that our palm/side prints are almost as unique as our fingerprints is a huge bonus for forensic experts, especially when any kind of handwritten paperwork is involved in a crime, and the database of those prints will solve several internationally renowned kidnappings and a few staged suicides by the year 2009.

Another type of database that will be in development by 2008 and commonly used among law enforcement agencies worldwide by 2014 will involve a specific, unique "fingerprint" of some sort within the iris of the human eye. Just as tiny iris-scanning cameras will someday be common security devices at ATMs and cash registers, in public buildings and airports, and in private residences, databases of iris images as part of our overall identification profile will help make the law-abiding population even more secure and make it even more difficult for criminals to find a place to hide.

Someone who manages to steal and use your ATM card and pin number, for example, will be sadly disappointed to discover that not only will the ATM's iris camera refuse to dispense cash to what it knows is the wrong eye, but the iris database will be triggered by a silent alarm and tell the police almost instantly the exact identity of whoever tried to steal money from your bank account. And good luck to anyone "on the run" who tries to use any form of public transportation, from planes to buses to trains to rented cars, all of which will be equipped with that same system of tiny cameras hooked up to a central iris database. The database will alert security and law enforcement to any would-be passengers who should be detained. Short of proof of an iris transplant, there won't be an easy way for criminals to claim that they've been unfairly mistaken for someone else.

The most complicated but invaluable law enforcement database to be developed in the first half of the twenty-first century will be the voice database. Between pitch, tone, rhythm, dialect, and countless other variables, the truth is that, like fingerprints, no two voices are absolutely identical, and the database that will take full advantage of that fact is going to be perfected in around 2025. The voice database will be able to detect the most subtle inflection, the tiniest hint of an accent, any number of differences between one voice and another that would be indiscernible to even the most sensitive human ear. It will be able to detect and eliminate any filters or synthesizers or other technological efforts to alter or disguise the voice, and no impersonator will be gifted enough to fool it.

There's a current, brilliantly effective investigative science called creative linguistics, which takes the art of document examining and forgery detecting to a whole new level. Creative linguistics is a means of studying the actual language style and often subtle idiosyncrasies a writer is known to use and then comparing them to a document alleged to have been written by that same writer. The results can be surprising, even if the handwriting itself appears to match perfectly or both documents were generated on identical typewriters or a computer.

Let's say the police are investigating a suspicious alleged suicide in which a lengthy note was left that gives every indication of having been written by the victim, right down to the handwriting and fingerprints. With the help of other documents known to have been written by the victim— personal letters, diaries, even hastily scribbled "to do" lists—a forensic linguist can do a comparison and see if the subtle styles and idiosyncrasies match. Did the victim tend to use a lot of contractions when writing, like "don't" and "aren't" and "haven't," or was the victim more likely to spell those words out into "do not" and "are not" and "have not"? Did the victim write more often in simple declarative sentences, or in compound sentences connected with a frequent use of conjunctions like "and" and "but"? Did the writing tend toward whole, grammatically correct sentences, like "I'm going on vacation," or did the victim use such "grammatical shorthand" as "Going on vacation"? To a skilled forensic linguist, those tiny stylistic details that even the most brilliant forger might overlook can be as conclusive as DNA when it comes to analyzing an alleged suicide note or any other suspicious document.

The voice database that will be perfected and in common international use by 2025 will include a computerized audio form of forensic linguistics, which will process speech patterns, styles and idiosyncrasies in every voice analysis. Not only will the database be able to identify the speaker, it will also be able to identify whether or not the speaker is using his or her own words (i.e., speech patterns) or reciting words prepared by someone else.

And in case you're wondering, not even a criminal with a true genius for affecting accents and inflections is likely to slip past the linguistic aspect of the voice database. Our speech patterns are so deeply ingrained in all of us that even when we cultivate an accent, lose an accent or speak fluently in a foreign language, we tend to maintain those same patterns and styles, those specific tiny details of the way we talk that, for reasons we neither think about anymore nor understand, simply sound "right" to our ear.

And so, by about 2025, when any criminal's voice is recorded during the commission of a crime, that recording will be entered into the database and the criminal will be identified by voice within minutes. By then surveillance cameras will record both video and audio on crystal-clear huge-capacity computer disks instead of grainy, recycled, silent videotape, which means any burglary, robbery or murder caught on camera will have a known suspect or suspects almost immediately, unless no one says a word for the duration of the crime. A ransom call from a kidnapper will tell the authorities exactly who the kidnapper is, and "anonymous" threatening or harassing phone calls of any kind won't stay anonymous long enough to be worth trying to get away with. This voice database will eventually be so readily accessible that, even if someone has managed to get their hands on the most personal information in the world about you, that person will never be able to succeed at identity theft over the phone. All the right answers to everything from your Social Security number to your mother's maiden name to the zip code of your billing address will mean nothing if it's not your voice that's giving those answers.

Long before 2025, though, a relative of this very sophisticated voice database will be perfected, for a different but equally invaluable purpose.

Lie Detection

As digital voice recording technology becomes more and more sensitive and highly advanced, its usefulness to law enforcement will expand into countless areas, not the least of which will be the development of a lie detector so accurate that its results, unlike lie detector results today, will finally be admissible in a court of law. It will work in tandem with other physiological monitoring devices, and it will somehow be able to measure vocal stress, excessive swallowing, audible changes in breathing patterns and other involuntary signs of possible deception. By 2012 these brilliant voice and physiological monitors will be combined into a polygraph device that will be both foolproof and 100 percent accurate.

Added to the physiological data that polygraphs already monitor, by the way, will be skin temperature and something to do with the dilation of the pupil of the eye, both of which apparently vary when someone is lying. Whatever the polygraph device of 2012 looks like and however it works, it will be able to record those changes as well, even if the subject chooses to take the lie detector test with eyes closed.

Surveillance and Emergency Alerts

Here's something that will come as a surprise to absolutely no one: the future of surveillance, law enforcement emergency alerts and dispatches, police pursuits and countless other forms of tracking down and apprehending criminals lies in satellite technology.

Let's get the downside out of the way first, the part that will go too far for a while and have to be reined in before its benefits to society outweigh its invasiveness. By

around 2015 virtually every home in the
United States will either have a satellite dish
or be accessible by a nearby satellite dish.
Through those satellite dishes, almost anyone in law enforcement or government will
have the technology to place the occupants
and visitors in that home under surveillance,
including their phone calls, computer activity, TV viewing habits, private conversations—you name it. In theory, search warrants will still be required for any and all of
this surveillance. In practice, of course, the
search warrant process will be frequently
sidestepped, abused or ignored completely
until society and the courts demand that
basic human rights and integrity take
precedence over technological bullying.

In the hands of responsible, dedicated
law enforcement personnel, though, the ongoing advancements of satellite technology
will be a blessing in any number of ways. By
around 2011 every new car will be manufactured with a satellite communication
system already installed, a highly advanced
version of the brilliant OnStar system that
exists today, and it will be impossible to dis-
able the system without practically disman-
tling the entire car. That same system will

be available for used cars as well, and hugely popular, since it will allow satellite TV reception in our cars, as if we aren't already distracted enough while we drive. But once a car is equipped with a satellite system, and the car's VIN number attached to that system, law enforcement will be able to pinpoint the location of cars that have been stolen or carjacked, or used in an abduction or an escape, or driven by a suspect who's under surveillance but hasn't been arrested yet. Law enforcement already uses satellite-controlled GPS (Global Positioning System) tracking, but by 2011 the system will be so advanced that they'll be able to simply turn off a targeted car via satellite once they're in position to make a safe capture and arrest.

(And while you're at it, car manufacturers, would you please spend the extra few dollars and minutes to install trunk releases *inside the trunk*? Aren't we a little too far along, technologically speaking, to hear of anyone being locked inside the trunk of a car anymore? How hard is that?)

Satellite communication will also play an enormous role in police dispatches, thanks to the upcoming ability of satellites to be so precise that they'll act as virtual neighborhood watchdogs and aerial eyewitnesses. Just as law enforcement will be able to tap into satellite signals for help in tracking and location, by 2014 satellites will also be able to send alerts to law enforcement that their help is needed, like a 9-1-1 call from space, much more quickly than any of us could ever even reach for the phone, let alone pick it up and dial it. And to settle the inevitable differences in eyewitness accounts of what happened once law enforcement does arrive on the scene, satellites will be able to instantly relay digital footage of the incident that triggered the alarm in the first place.

To give law enforcement one more added edge, by 2015 their custom-designed high-speed vehicles will be atomically powered and capable of becoming airborne enough to fly several feet above other traffic. Not only will they be able to get to the scene of a crime or accident in a matter of moments, but they'll also be impossible for criminals to outrun. Any attempt to steal one of these amazing vehicles will be futile, by the way, since they'll only be operable by a handful of law enforcement personnel whose DNA codes have been programmed into the computerized ignition system.

Public Involvement

While law enforcement and forensics are becoming more sophisticated and interactive throughout the world, the world community in general will become more sophisticated, vigilant and cooperative about crime fighting as well, and even more passionate about demanding their right to safe, secure, peaceful lives. We know that even with the best technology has to offer, the police will continue to be underpaid and outnumbered, which is where the public will come in with increasing effectiveness, not as outlaw vigilantes as potentially dangerous as the criminals they're after, but as a united force working hand in hand with law enforcement to reclaim the streets.

I've never been shy about expressing my admiration for John Walsh and his brave insistence on turning personal tragedy into the triumph of television's *America's Most Wanted,* in which viewers' tips help solve crimes. By 2009 there will be an international version of John Walsh's show, actually a twenty-four-hour-a-day, seven-day-a-week satellite channel, funded by governments, private donations and smart sponsors around the world, that will expose a nonstop parade of wanted criminals in every corner of the globe to an audience of countless millions. Tiplines and websites will be more than equipped to handle the constant flow of responses from that vast global audience, and it will be perpetually reassuring to see proof over and over again that most people who share this planet really do want to participate in making a difference if they're just given a concrete way to go about it.

All of which adds up to a simple truth we can count on, even in the ugliest, darkest, most chaotic times: in the long run, as it always has been and always will be, whether it's here on earth or anywhere else in the universe, God sees to it that the "good guys" have a whole lot more to look forward to than the "bad guys" every single time.

PART III

OUR PHYSICAL, EMOTIONAL, MENTAL AND SPIRITUAL HEALTH

CHAPTER TWELVE

Health and Medicine

The worlds of health and medicine have been lifelong passions of mine. I treasure my friendships with some of the most highly respected members of the medical community, and I'm very proud of my reciprocal referral relationships with literally hundreds of physicians around the world.

At the same time, I can't stress enough that while I'm fairly well read on the subjects of health and medicine, I have no formal education in those areas, no degrees and no medical certificates or licenses, and I'm certainly not qualified to prescribe medication of any kind. I've given thousands upon thousands of psychic health readings in my fifty-plus professional years. I'm very specific when I find some physical or physi-ological problem I'm concerned about in a client. Those specifics invariably include checkups and tests from trusted, reputable, fully accredited doctors, most of whom know a whole lot more about health and medicine after all those years of studying than the rest of us would even want to. But you'll never hear me recommend any "med-ication" that can't be bought over the counter at your nearest health food store, and you'll certainly never hear me suggest that you run home and start experimenting with a variety of powders, pills, procedures and untested "miracle cures." I wouldn't fol-low an idiotic suggestion like that myself, so why on earth would I ask you to?

In case you're wondering, there's a rea-son I'm carrying on about the importance of listening to qualified experts and avoiding the temptation to experiment with some-thing as priceless as our health. The pages that follow contain prophecies in the areas of health and medicine. They're not in-tended to be anything *but* prophecies. I don't want it entering your mind as you read this chapter to try something on your own that seems as if it might be worth experimenting with. In other words, to quote an over-used and over-ignored warning, "Don't try this at home."

The Aura Scanner

I'm sure most of you are familiar with the word "aura," which refers to the emanation of energy that all living things emit. In the next five years, the worlds of medicine and parapsychology will become more and more intertwined, and one of the results will be the introduction in high-tech doctors' offices of "aura scanners" in approximately 2008.

I can't resist mentioning that I once shared a speaking engagement in San Francisco with Dr. Thelma Moss of UCLA. Her extensive work with auras included Kirlian photography, or actual photographs of energy emanations from everything from plants to the renowned Soviet paranormalist Uri Geller, and in my excitement to meet her I quietly shared this prophecy about the aura scanner. To her credit, she didn't laugh in my face, she simply smiled and said,

"Sylvia, I believe you totally, but I won't be around to see it." That was in the 1980s. Dr. Moss died in 1997. She's very much around, though, I know that, having a high old time on the Other Side watching me finally commit to paper what I said to her twenty years ago, that the aura scanner will be a reality someday.

If I had told you in, let's say, those same 1980s that the day would come when you'd lie down on a bed in your doctor's office and be inserted into a great big tube that would scan your whole body in a matter of minutes, you would probably have said, "Poor Sylvia, maybe a nice long vacation would help." But of course a bed inserted into a great big tube is exactly what the invaluable and widely used MRI is. In an MRI, or Magnetic Resonance Imaging scan, a combination of magnetic fields, radio waves, computers and our bodies' own hydrogen atoms produces images of an amazing array of diseases, tumors, inflammations, traumas, swelling, bleeding and any number of other internal problems that might never have been detected with a less sophisticated form of examination.

The aura scanner will essentially be a

more highly developed version of the MRI. Instead of lying on a bed, the patient will stand on a slowly rotating disc, while what appears to be a kind of infrared light scans the body from front to back and from side to side, looking for irregularities in the body's aura. Again, remember that the aura is an emanation of energy, like an electrical charge given off by the body. In this first phase of the examination, the scanner will simply detect interruptions, "power surges" or other abnormalities in that halo of energy. The scanning light will stop at the precise spot where it finds an abnormality in the aura, and the corresponding image of the patient's body on the scanner's computer will mark that spot as an area to be examined more closely.

Once the first phase of the aura scanner's exam is complete and the body's areas of illness and/or potential vulnerability have been identified, the second phase of the scanner's work begins. That same light moves to each of the marked abnormalities in the aura and, by changing colors, diagnoses the time sensitivity of the problem it's detected. Let's say, for example, that during the first phase of the exam, the aura scanner marked a spot on the patient's chest. The light will now move back to that spot during the second phase for a closer look. If the light changes to red, the problem is urgent, potentially life-threatening and needs immediate attention—a tumor, severely blocked coronary arteries or other major heart abnormalities, a previously unde-tected embolism or blood clot, and so on. If the light changes to green, the problem is serious but less urgent—pneumonia, heart disease or cystic fibrosis, for example. If the light becomes yellow, there's a nonurgent, nonthreatening disturbance at work, maybe a bronchial infection or even just a harmless functional heart murmur.

The range of light codes will obviously continue to expand as the technology of the aura scanner continues to expand. But from the moment of its acceptance in the med-ical world, the scanner will save us from more wasted time and money, frustration, guesswork, misdiagnoses, misprescribed medications and unnecessary testing and lab work than we can begin to calculate.

I also can't resist smiling at the fact that even the most skeptical, closed-minded doctors and patients, many of whom will insist that auras don't even exist to begin with, will find it impossible to argue with the infallible accuracy of the aura scanner. Hypochondriacs will have an even harder time convincing their doctors that something is wrong with them when two or three aura scanner exams in a row proceed without the light pausing on any part of their body even once. And patients with legitimate complaints will finally have a reliable alternative to those rare, infuriating doctors who, because they're either lazy or inept, keep saying, "You're perfectly healthy, it's all in your head." The aura scanner will make it very clear very quickly whether it's the doctor or the patient who knows what he or she is talking about.

Cancer

The despicable scourge of cancer has been plaguing humankind for longer than we'll ever know. The first commonly acknowledged written description of it dates back to around 1600 B.C. And I'll never forget a brilliant man named Dr. Zahi Hawas, who's the head of the Giza Archaeological

Department in Egypt, telling me that many mummies removed from ancient Egyptian pyramids were revealed in autopsies to have died from cancer. The word "cancer" itself, in fact, was coined by Hippocrates, the Greek physician known as the "Father of Medicine," who died in 370 B.C. It's an ageless, awesome, viciously arrogant disease, which makes it all the more humbling to know that many of us will have the privilege of witnessing its downfall.

I have to repeat a couple of things again before I say what I'm about to say. One is that I'm not a doctor, I don't pretend to be and I can't offer any technical medical explanations beyond the information I'm given. The other is that I'll consider it a very personal betrayal if you use anything you read in this or any other book of mine as an excuse to harm yourself or anyone else. I have no self-help to offer toward a cure for cancer. Believe me, I wish I did.

That having been said, I'm fascinated that something as insidious as cancer is going to be fought with something just as insidious. If there's one thing we know about cancer cells, it's that they're insatiably greedy, and that they destroy by devouring the healthy cells around them. What the worlds of science and medicine will provide in the future is a way for them to satisfy their greed and, in the process, end up actually destroying themselves.

In approximately 2006, a handful of highly specialized oncologists will begin injecting the nuclei of cancer cells in the body with the most powerful addictive drugs available at that time, as addictive as heroin or Oxy-Contin are now. Within a very few treatments the nuclei of these specific diseased cells will be addicted themselves and in search of more of that drug. Unable to find it in healthy cells or anywhere else but within their own cell structure, they'll desperately resort to feeding off of themselves and one another for their "fix," until the induced addiction makes them literally self-destruct and eradicate themselves.

Not only will this very precise microscopic surgery become more widely used over the years, but the theory behind it will find its way into more areas of life-saving research as well, including, believe it or not, more effective treatment of addictions themselves.

Paralysis

There's great news right around the corner for those who suffer from partial or extreme paralysis. Instead of the electrodes that currently just stimulate the muscles, there will be computer chips implanted at the base of the brain that will send precise signals to both muscles and nerves. These chips will duplicate the communication among the brain, the muscular system, and the intricate network of nerves throughout the body that has somehow broken down, allowing signals to flow freely again to their intended receivers and for movement to return.

The imagery I get, if it helps, is a lineman replacing a fallen power pole beside a dark house. Once the new pole is strongly in place and the electrical lines are properly attached to it, the lights come on throughout the house again. The computer chip that's coming will act as these electrical lines attached to a strong new pole, returning power to a dark house, i.e., movement to an immobilized body.

And again, it's right around the corner, at the end of 2004 and the beginning of 2005.

Immune Deficiencies

I wish this weren't going to take until around 2008, because the handful of doctors I know who already feel as passionately about it as I do are having great success with it among their clients. The medical mainstream still feels compelled to drag its feet, debate, argue or, in some cases, take the exact opposite position, though, so it looks as if 2008 is about the best we can hope for.

It will be accepted in that year and put to good use that all autoimmune-related illnesses respond dramatically to a high-protein diet. Proteins are great cell builders and insulators, and those properties will be mined into solid gold as research continues. Even now, everything from candida to chronic fatigue syndrome to fibromyalgia is improved when the diet is designed around an essential, generous core of protein. Diabetes and hypoglycemia (low blood sugar), unrelated as they are to the immune system, are often responsive to high-protein diets as well. What we know now about the power of proteins is only a glimmer of what's to come, and if someone decides to prove me wrong and make these break-throughs happen sooner than 2008, I'll per-sonally lead the standing ovation.

Also on the horizon, by probably 2013 or 2014, is great success with the use of hu-man growth hormone for the treatment of ALS (Lou Gehrig's disease), muscular dys-trophy and multiple sclerosis. I would love to be more specific, but the connection be-tween that hormone and those illnesses is all I have at the moment. The instant I have more, I'll shout it from the rooftops to every doctor, scientist and researcher who'll lis-ten, you can count on it.

Stem Cell Research

Stem cells are basically cells that are able to restore themselves for extended periods of time by means of cell division, and they can be manipulated, by our bodies or in ex-perimental laboratory situations, to perform specific functions. Stem cells can be "taught," for example, to become the cells that make a heart muscle beat, or the cells that create digestive fluids in the stomach.

Their value to the human body is incalculable, as is their potential in the areas of biological and medical research. Experiments on embryonic stem cells from mice and from human adults have been going on for decades, with strong indications that expanding on those experiments could lead to cures for everything from Parkinson's disease to diabetes to birth defects to heart disease to cancer to leukemia, and on and on.

And then, in 1998, as you're probably aware, researchers discovered how to extract stem cells from human embryos and grow them in a laboratory environment, igniting a firestorm of impassioned controversy. On one side stand those in favor of stem cell research, pleading for the untold millions of bodies that might be healed and lives that might be saved as a direct result of the research. On the other side stand those opposed and even horrified by the idea of stem cell research, pleading for the helpless, voiceless embryos whose lives they consider sacrosanct.

The intensely emotional debate over stem cell research will rage on until around late 2005 or into 2006, when researchers

will be able, with perfectly clear con-
sciences and no harm to the human em-
bryo, to successfully extract stem cells from
the umbilical cord and proceed with the
thrilling advancements stem cell research
has to offer. Not only will it lead to an exciting explosion of life-saving cures, but in the
year 2012 it will also result in the ability to
actually exchange old body parts for com-
patible new ones, so that finally the mythi-
cal fountain of youth will become a reality.

And if we think the medical community is
too riddled with fakes and charlatans now,
just wait till those fountain-of-youth injections and surgeries hit the market. Please
remember that with each new fantastic
medical development there will be frauds
gathering like vultures waiting to cash in on
it without a care in the world as to how they
might be jeopardizing or even destroying
people's lives. I'm sure the FDA, the AMA
and all state licensing boards do their best
to ensure excellence when it comes to the
medical community and drugs at our dis-
posal (actually, I'm not sure of that at all, I'm
just trying to be polite), but the real responsibility for checking credentials and refusing
to settle for anything or anyone less than

the best, most qualified, most legitimate and most highly recommended is *ours.*

Help for the Ears and Eyes

By the year 2020 researchers will have created a wonderful new synthetic material, made from three currently existing materials I can't quite get the names of. What's thrilling about this synthetic is that it will be able to perfectly duplicate the eardrum and will be routinely implanted, to restore hearing to countless thousands.

In the meantime, long before 2020, blindness will become a thing of the past. Organ transplants will continue to be great contributors to the elimination of blindness and will increase in the coming years. But in addition, a tiny digital device will be developed that, when implanted in the frontal lobes of the brain, will create or reestablish communication between the brain and the eyes. From the instant the device is in place and activated, the eyes will perceive shapes, colors and light, much like a newborn baby when its eyes first open. As the brain learns that the device is useful, and enables it to do something it inherently knows it was meant to do, it will quickly accelerate its progress and achieve full normal vision, from a starting place of total blindness, in just a matter of days.

The Common Cold

This won't thrill the drug companies, which are making a fortune off of over-the-counter medications, but the common cold will be over with by about 2009 or 2010. And I guess when you think about it, it makes all the sense in the world that the eventual solution to the common cold will involve heat. One of the body's first responses when a cold hits, after all, is to develop a fever. Body temperature rises as the body does battle with the invading bacteria, and obviously we know that heat kills bacteria or we wouldn't automatically start boiling water every time we want to sterilize something. Many doctors I've spoken to in the last couple of years have confirmed that they're not as quick as they used to be to prescribe fever-reducing medication unless a patient's body temperature is dangerously high. Their logic is that the body's own built-in immune system arsenal, with heat as one of its "biggest guns," should be given a chance to do its job, with medication to supplement it rather than to completely take over for it. And they're not wrong. The more our own immune systems are allowed to participate in healing us, the more quickly we're healed.

Now, I wish I had more specifics to offer on this, because I'd love to help speed things along by a few years. But all I've got for the time being is a small cubicle that will become a common fixture in most doctors' offices, which will be heated to a very precise temperature and perhaps infused with an antibiotic vapor of some kind. We'll stand inside the cubicle for five or six minutes, and a combination of the carefully regulated atmosphere in the cubicle and our own body temperature will destroy the rhinitis germ that causes a vast percentage of the common colds we all suffer from. And because the rhinitis germ is also the culprit behind many allergies and asthma complications, this cubicle/heat approach will branch into cures for any number of other currently "incurable" breathing disorders and diseases.

Again, it looks to me as if we won't be seeing these breakthroughs become available and readily accessible until about 2009 or 2010. Until then, what can I say, drink plenty of fluids, get lots of bed rest, take echinacea and goldenseal and vitamin C until you feel as if they're coming out your ears and just hang in there as best you can.

Traditional Surgery

The transformations we have to look forward to in the world of surgery are nothing short of thrilling. By the year 2015 invasive surgery involving cutting and scalpels and stitches and scars will be virtually unheard of. In its place we'll see applications of laser surgery that will make today's laser surgery look simplistic—almost as simplistic as my attempt to describe these images without the technical expertise or vocabulary to go into detail or explain the procedures.

The intense, precise beam of laser light we're already familiar with will be enhanced by 2015 by a computerized sensor, a kind of "electronic eye" that will not only be pre-programmed to perform whatever procedure is needed but also be able to locate any other abnormalities in the area of the surgery, analyze them in a matter of seconds and take whatever actions are medically appropriate based on the computerized sensor's analysis. The precision of the beam and any procedures it performs will leave all the healthy tissue surrounding the affected area untouched, there will be no incisions to heal afterward, and the postsurgical recovery time will be minimal and virtually pain-free.

Transplants and Transfusions

In around 2025, it will become routine for all of us, when we're very young children, to have cells taken from each of our major organs and stored "on file" for future reference in the event that we ever need one of those organs replaced. Cloning will have progressed so dramatically by then that creating a new liver, for example, from a few of our own liver cells will be routine, and the agonizing waiting lists for organ donors will be fading memories. So, thank God, will the horrifying sales of organs on the black market, where people's fear and desperation are exploited to such a heartbreaking extreme.

2025 is also the year in which synthetic blood will be perfected and be heralded as one of the millennium's most significant medical breakthroughs to date. Beyond being universal in type so that it can be safely used in any and all transfusions, it will also contain added nutritional and immune system supplements. Transfusions of this synthetic blood, in other words, will go far beyond restoring the body with a fresh, healthy supply of blood. They'll actually enhance the health of the body far beyond its condition before the transfusion and continue enhancing it long after the transfusion has taken place, as these added supplements circulate through every organ, limb and cell.

For Women Only

If I thought it would do the slightest bit of good, and if it weren't so painfully obvious, I would spend a couple of paragraphs venting about how if men had to go through yeast infections, cramps, PMS, menstrual periods, chronic water retention and menopause, the medical world would have eradicated every one of those things a hundred years ago. But far be it from me to be bitter, so instead, I'll stay focused on the future of yet another experience strictly limited to us females—harsh and unfair as it may be.

As women become able to conceive and bear children at increasingly advanced ages, they're going to want and need more regular, high-tech prenatal care. While all women benefit significantly from diligent prenatal care, older mothers-to-be in particular will be a compelling impetus behind a technology that will become common and a literal Godsend by 2010. We know that some amazing surgeries are already being performed on fetuses in the womb, which is enough to make me weep with awe as it is. But by 2010, to keep a special eye on the higher-risk pregnancies of more mature women, ultrasound and amniocentesis will be more specifically diagnostic than ever, allowing truly miraculous fetal injections that can actually correct genetic deficien-

cies and prevent some birth defects and illnesses before they happen.

Questions come up from time to time
about whether or not we're "playing God" in
situations like that. I'm truly mystified that
anyone would wonder. God created doctors
too, after all, and the scientists and researchers and everyone else responsible
for every discovery that leads to such miracles as fetal surgeries and the prenatal correction of genetic deficiencies. As far as I'm
concerned, we'd be doing a terrible disservice to God if we had the skill, the talent
and the technology but lacked the compassion to try everything in our power to help a
child be born as healthy and whole as possible.

2010 will also usher in the reemergence
of birthing chambers, which will be developed for the benefit of both mothers and
babies going through the rigorous process
of childbirth. Inspired by our ancestors, who
knew enough to take full advantage of the
law of gravity, birthing chambers will involve
a pulley system that allows the woman to
give birth while being suspended from an
overhanging series of strong, padded, comfortable straps. When the baby is born, it

drops *down* from the mother, as gravity prefers, into waiting soft, sterile pillows in the hands of the doctor and nurse in attendance.

Of equal importance, the atmosphere of the birthing chambers will lend itself to tranquillity, relaxation and peace of mind. The walls of the small circular rooms will act as screens on which natural meditative imagery of mountains, meadows, gardens, the ocean, or any collage of the mother's choice will be projected. Gentle music of woodwinds and the quiet tide will be piped in, lights will be dimmed before the mother ever arrives in the chamber, and aromatherapy will be put to subtle use throughout the birth. The emphasis for the mother will be on childbirth as a reverent experience rather than a clinical one, and the infant will be born into at least some pale stab at a replica of the magnificent beauty it just left behind on the Other Side, rather than the rubber gloves, cold tile, bright lights and stainless steel it's unceremoniously hurled into now, with no warning at all.

Oh, and by the way, even before 2010— probably in around 2008—don't be alarmed if you discover that the placenta is being saved and carefully preserved by the hospital. Let's face it, you're through with it, and your baby is through with it, so by all means, be happy that it's going to a good cause: it will have been found by then that there's a nutrient or protein complex in the placenta that somehow slows the progress of Alzheimer's disease.

You see? Right down to the placenta, it's just give, give, give with us. (Okay, I'm finished being long-suffering now. We can include the men again.)

Medications

Even now, responsible drug companies are hard at work on forms of medication that the body can assimilate more quickly and effectively than ever. That research will continue and expand until, by around 2014, pills, capsules and even most liquid medicine will be replaced by readily accessible vaporized heat and oxygen chambers that can infuse every pore of the body with the recommended medications. Electrodes and some kind of electronic synthesizer will be used to relieve pain and stimulate healing for most injuries. And the same technology used in today's MRIs, which incorporates the effects of magnets on the human body, will be used not only to reduce inflammations but also to regulate any problematic rhythms of the heart.

As most of you know, Botox injections are currently enjoying great popularity in the cosmetics world as a way to "freeze" very specific muscles in the face and, as a result, eliminate wrinkles in those areas for several weeks or months, until the effect wears off. Have I ever had Botox injections? Absolutely. Have I ever had them anywhere but in a doctor's office, administered by a fully licensed, board-certified physician? Not a chance, and I never will. Not with a gun to my head would I let anyone without a medical degree stick needles in my face, let alone inject a toxin into it. And Botox is a toxin, actually a protein produced by bacteria. It's a prescription drug. Next time you get invited to a "Botox party," or hear about a salon that's offering free introductory Botox injections with every pedicure, insist on seeing the credentials of the person who's giving the injections. If there's no medical degree and license among those credentials, run. I don't care how much money you're supposedly saving by not bothering with that pesky "doctor" detail. What kind of bargain is it if you end up with your face infected, swollen from an allergic reaction and/or paralyzed in all the wrong places for three or four months until the effects wear off?

There. Now. About the future of Botox, which is exciting. As early as the end of 2004, Botox applications will become useful in the treatment of arthritis and severe back problems. Not long after that, they will be developed to treat swollen glands, broken bones and torn cartilage and tendons.

In other words, like so many prescription drugs, misused or used carelessly, Botox can be a nightmare. But in the right hands, under the right conditions, the benefits we already appreciate will turn out to be only a glimpse of what it can do.

Arthritis, by the way, will become a minor annoyance at its worst by the beginning of 2007, thanks to another medication that will both relieve pain and restore the affected nerves and muscles. I don't know the name of the medication or the name of the plant from which it will be made. What I do know is that the plant grows in the Amazon rain forest. It's a flowering plant that resembles a cactus but technically isn't one, and the milky substance it secretes will provide the base for a number of healing medications, much like aloe but far more effective.

The rain forests will be yielding any number of other marvelous medicinal secrets as well in the next three years—yet another reason why we've got to stop treating the rain forests as if they're expendable, and/or ours to destroy in the first place. For example, as the natives there already know and we'll be learning soon, there's also a large-leafed plant hidden deep in the Amazon rain forest that looks like an elephant's ear plant on steroids. The substance that flows through its thick stems is clear and more like a gel than a liquid. That substance will turn out to be invaluable for the treatment of chronic sores on the body that have resisted all other traditional approaches. When applied directly to the sores, it will cause instantaneous pain relief, an immediate stop to bleeding and swelling and a healing so accelerated that the images I'm getting of it almost look like time-lapse photography.

There's a vaccination breakthrough coming in 2005 that will essentially be the human equivalent of the parvo vaccine I get for my beloved dogs, especially when they're puppies. The parvovirus in dogs was first discovered in 1978. It's a virus that thrives in rapidly growing cells, which is why puppies are affected more often than adult dogs, and it's also hardy enough to survive for months outside the body in a completely unprotected environment. So what does that have to do with us humans? Well, is it me, or doesn't that definition of the parvovirus bear more than a passing resemblance to a description of the AIDS virus? Again, maybe it *is* me, since by no stretch of the imagination am I a doctor or qualified to make a reliably valid pronouncement about a connection between parvo and AIDS. If that connection exists, though, and we can vaccinate our dogs against parvo, then how big a leap can it be to a human vaccine against AIDS? It won't surprise you that I've asked several of my physician friends about this. Their replies have all been some variation on the following: "The vaccines currently being researched are still in the experimental stage and in their present form might be fatal." Hello?! And AIDS *isn't* fatal?!

At any rate, the good news is, there will be a significant vaccine breakthrough for humans against HIV/AIDS in 2005, nonfatal and a Godsend, believe me.

Last but by no means least, in 2040 a truly amazing plant extract will be discovered in New Zealand. The name of the plant sounds like "chimunga." This miraculous extract will somehow stimulate the production of new brain cells and ultimately enable the brain to comprehend, retain and process information faster than any currently known computer. Humankind's "new and improved brain" will give birth to a worldwide flood of innovations, breakthroughs, solutions and cures in every aspect of life, making even our most earnest and significant efforts to date look primitive by comparison.

I'm an American, and I'm so proud and in awe of the brilliant, tireless, passionate and indisputably humanitarian scientists, researchers and physicians the United States has to offer. I'm also very often frustrated, on their behalf and on ours, at the politics and bureaucracy and small-minded, self-interested "public policy" that can keep the flood of contributions from those brilliant minds down to a relative trickle. Once health care and research funding in America are treated as the essential priorities they really are, and the inane time- and money-wasting snarl of bureaucratic red tape is reduced to simple, fair, sensible and safety-conscious guidelines, the United States will be the global leader it already could be in the world of medicine. Until then, we shouldn't be surprised at the number of Americans who, when they find themselves in a serious health crisis, end up heading to Europe, and particularly Sweden and Switzerland, for the help that should be readily available much, much closer to home.

The Downside

I also see some health crises ahead, and as always when it comes to bad news, nobody will be happier than I if it turns out I'm wrong.

* Certain strains of the flu, as well as the SARS virus, will create more dev-

astation in 2004, particularly in the Orient and in South America. A vaccine that somehow comes from chickens and pigs will ultimately put an end to these particular viruses, and in the meantime one of our best protections against them will be the daily use of good over-the-counter antioxidants. (And here's an added note I don't pretend to understand, but since I promised not to edit myself about these things, I'll mention that for some reason, a particularly effective antioxidant against these oncoming viruses can be found in artichokes.)

* Between now and the end of 2006 or the beginning of 2007, despite upcoming vaccines and the strides we've seen in medication and general knowledge in recent years, the HIV/AIDS virus will surge again even more viciously than before in certain third world areas of South America, Mexico, Africa and Asia.

Part of this will be due to the tragic fact that many of the medications and much of the growing awareness of these diseases we've seen aren't reaching these people, which is simply inhumane and unacceptable. Some of it will also be due to the obscene spread of *mis*information, for no apparent purpose other than some political agenda I don't even care to theorize about. One example of deliberate misinformation was published as recently as October of 2003. I won't perpetuate it by quoting it, nor will I drive the Dutton legal department insane by specifying the source of this astonishing misstatement of facts. But in case the immediate, appropriate correction and "shame on you!" from the World Health Organization and countless other responsible medical and humanitarian agencies didn't clarify things enough, I want to chime in with the truth as well, for whatever the added sound of my voice is worth: *If you're sexually active, latex condoms are not only effective but absolutely essential in helping to stop the spread of AIDS.*

✳ In 2010 another illness related to immune system deficiencies will arrive. It seems to be connected to exotic birds imported from Brazil and is transmitted from the birds to us humans by tiny mites of some kind. This insidious bacterial infection will manifest itself in the form of a funguslike growth on the body that's resistant to all medications and antibiotics known at that time and will resemble the "flesh-eating disease" of several years ago, on a much wider scale. It will be so highly contagious that those who are infected will have to be quarantined, and there will be four or five years of panic before some combination of electrical currents and extreme heat will be found to destroy the fungus and the bacteria that's causing it.

✳ By 2020 we'll see more people than ever wearing surgical masks and rubber gloves in public, inspired by an outbreak of a severe pneumonia-like illness that attacks both the lungs and the bronchial tubes and is ruthlessly resistant to treatment. This illness will be particularly baffling in that, after causing a winter of absolute panic, it will seem to vanish completely until ten years later, making both its source and its cure that much more mysterious.

Surgical masks and rubber gloves are fine in high-risk environments, and God knows I'm a varsity cheerleader on the subject of personal hygiene—bathe or shower every day, wash your hair every day, don't even think about using the toilet without washing your hands immediately afterward, brush your teeth at least twice a day—you name the basics and I both believe in them and do them myself. The trick is to know where to draw the line between healthy cleanliness and obsessive-compulsive disorder, in which you're more terrified of germs than many children are of monsters hiding under their beds, and cower your way through life instead of getting out there and living it. I wandered a little too close to that line myself once, and I learned a lesson I'm happy to pass along for a little added perspective.

When I gave birth to my first child, Paul, I was determined to be the most perfect mother any baby ever had, especially when it came to his health. No germ was going to get near my helpless little Paul, not if I could help it. In short, if anything was going to come within a three-foot radius of him, I sterilized it. If I could boil it (bottles, nipples, pacifiers, bibs, clothes, toys, diapers, even his diaper pins), I boiled it. If it was too big to boil (his bedding, his crib mattress, his "binky"), I washed it in scalding-hot water. I'm not sure a day went by when I wasn't scrubbing his crib, the floor, the sink I bathed him in—I hope you've got the idea by now, because I'm worn out just remembering all this. And my great reward for those exhaustive nonstop efforts was that every time I turned around, Paul seemed to have another cold, or the flu again, which would send me into a panic and make me even more compulsive about sterilizing his environment, if that was possible.

On about my eleventy billionth trip to our dear family doctor because Paul had sniffled once or something, I described my exhaustively flawless approach to germ-free motherhood and then sat waiting for sympathy, a medal, a testimonial dinner in my honor, I'm not sure what, while Dr. Carrier gaped at me. Finally he simply asked, "Sylvia, for God's sake, when are you going to let this poor baby build up his immune system?"

He wasn't wrong. I didn't go from hyper-sterile to slovenly with Paul, but I definitely lightened up, and by the time my second child, Chris, was born, I was letting him play with unboiled toys and wear washed but unboiled clothes. By the grace of God and Dr. Carrier, what do you know, both of my sons grew up healthy and strong as horses in spite of me.

Hardly a scientific experiment conducted by an expert, and I'm most certainly not making a case for exposing babies to as much bacteria as possible. I'm just saying that when it comes to life on earth, ex-tremes in almost any area, even a "perfect" germ-free environment, invariably end up doing more harm than good.

Quality of Life, Quality of Death

I have to bring up this subject again be-cause it's so important, and because it was in the "For Women Only" section, which means you men didn't just turn the page to avoid it, you ran screaming in case we were going to go into some of those things that embarrass you into complete senseless-ness.

With all the extraordinary strides ahead in health and the world of medicine, I know the question will come up repeatedly about the point at which humankind is "playing God." My answer to that will always be what it's always been: we all come to earth from the Other Side with certain gifts, and it's part of our contract with God to put those gifts to their best, most loving possi-ble use while we're here. When that use is manifested in the form of doctors, scientists and researchers whose work ultimately makes our lives richer, better, stronger, wiser, more active, longer or more purpose-ful, then who are we to judge who's "playing God" or who's simply acting on their con-tract with Him, with the mind He gave them and the knowledge He infused it with? God, after all, made doctors too. I just hope we'll never become too small-minded and judg-mental about medical breakthroughs to re-member that.

I also hope we'll always keep our spiritu-ality intact enough that it never becomes our goal, and the goal of the medical community, to cling to life on earth at all cost, regardless of quality and purpose, as if this is the only existence we'll ever have. By around 2050, the average human life span will have extended to somewhere between 120 and 130 years. That might sound unlikely unless you're aware that in 1900 it was 48 years and by 2000 it had increased significantly, to 79.7 years. Lives averaging well over a century long could be wonderful if they sustained their vitality, and if those many, many years of knowledge, wisdom and experience could be used to their maximum advantage. But let's face it, if we only define life as a body continuing to perform a handful of its most basic functions, those lives could also be nightmares, for us and for our loved ones.

Our lives on this earth, no matter how briefly or how long they last, are just moments in the context of the eternity God breathed into us at the instant He created us. Our real lives, joyful and glorious and perfect, are back Home, on the Other Side, where we all came from, the place we're wistfully Homesick for every minute we're here whether we're consciously aware of it or not, and where we'll go when we abandon these flawed, cumbersome bodies and soar Home again as alive as ever. Clinging fiercely to this one life, as if it's all there is and all there will ever be, would be no different than clinging fiercely to one random day of school, as if there's nowhere else to go but there and nothing more to learn.

I had an experience a few years ago that is sadly all too common. My father, whom I adored, was lying in a hospital bed, eighty-seven years old and in his final hours on earth after losing a hard-fought battle with cancer. I'd been by his side for weeks, exhausted, hating my inability to save him or trade places with him, trying to balance my profound love for him, which could celebrate his upcoming trip Home, with my selfish grief at the thought of a day on this earth without his laugh, the comfort of his voice and just the feeling I always had when Daddy was in the room that everything would be okay. I knew from his sad dark eyes that he was in agony despite his morphine drip, and I also knew he'd never be getting up and walking out of this hospital with me again.

"Sylvie?" he whispered. (Not a typo—that's what he called me.)

"What is it, Daddy?"

"Please get me out of this pain," he said.

It was such a simple, reasonable request, and not one a stoic like my father would ever have made unless the pain was becoming unbearable. I was in such a fog that to this day I only vaguely remember racing into the hallway and somehow finding the doctor. But I remember every word of our brief encounter as if it just happened five minutes ago.

"My father is suffering too much," I urgently told the doctor. "You've got to give him more morphine."

His tone was patient and measured with well-practiced good-bedside-manner calm. "But, Ms. Browne," he explained by rote, "we don't want him to get addicted."

He was serious, and I lost it. I'm sure they heard me scream in every hallway and room of that hospital. "Addicted?! He's dying, you imbecile!"

Without batting an eyelash, the doctor simply rubbed his chin and replied, "Yes, well, that is a problem."

Daddy got his added morphine, and after what seemed like a barbarically long time the muscles of his frail body relaxed and a painless peace eased across his face. He was gone a few short hours later.

As I said, I've heard variations on that story from clients and friends a thousand times ever since, and it will always send a quick, aching jolt through my heart. Which is why I'm especially appreciative of the fact that by about 2012 a strong drug will be developed, solely for irreversibly terminal patients, that will be administered in the form of a kind of time-release injection and allow them to be both pain-free and mentally lucid, as opposed to the either/or choice today's drugs demand. Ultimately, as the time-release effects proceed, both the body and the mind will very gradually and gently float off into a quiet, pain-free sleep—not so much the false euphoria current pain medications simulate but more like an actual, profound out-of-body meditation during which, if it wants, the spirit can slip joyfully through the tunnel to God's light, knowing its last moments on earth were filled with happiness and clarity for its loved ones to remember and cherish.

Special thanks in advance from a whole lot of us to whoever comes up with that one.

CHAPTER THIRTEEN

Diet, Fitness and the Way We Look

About forty years ago my Spirit Guide, Francine, for reasons I don't remember, was giving me a good talking to about some up-coming misconceptions concerning diet and nutrition. "There are going to be a lot of foolish generalizations," she said. "Like the idea that salt is bad, when it can be benefi-cial for people with low blood pressure, or an overreaction against protein, which can lead to iron deficiency and anemia. I'll tell you what the real killer is, what everyone would benefit from eliminating from their diet, and that's sugar." White, brown, raw, powdered—Francine didn't care what color it was, what form it came in or how great it tasted, it was as self-destructive as many other addictions as far as she was concerned. She was worried about it forty years ago, and she's still worried about it today.

It especially delights me, then, that in 2005 there will finally be some serious changes in the labeling and public understanding of the food we buy and eat. For example, it's currently common practice and perfectly legal to label certain foods "low-fat" and "non-fat" that are loaded with sugar, since technically sugar isn't a fat. It's impossible to calculate how many people are buying these low-fat and non-fat foods with the best healthy, dietetic intentions and wondering why they're not losing weight, and probably even gaining it. It's a dirty trick, and in 2005 an added prominent warning label about a "high sugar content" will be required instead of the small-print mention of it in the general "nutritional content" breakdown on the back of the package. In the meantime, just as drug companies now have to adhere to more stringent "truth in advertising" laws by listing possible negative side effects on their packaging and in TV ads, food companies will have to meet their version of those same demands. TV ads in particular will no longer be able to show people happily eating oversized meals or gigantic burgers they can barely fit in their mouths without also stating, out loud, the amount of sugar, carbohydrates and calories in the food they've just urged the public to run out and buy. Let's face it, we learn a lot from television, both good and bad. Starting in 2005 we'll start getting a lot more of our nutritional education from commercials, to the chagrin of some food companies, which would rather not be made to reveal quite so much about what they're selling.

By late in 2006 or early 2007 there will be more and more emphasis on the realization that overeating is often due not to a sense of feeling hungry but to a sense of feeling unsatisfied. And a significant part of that problem will be solved by easily adminis-tered daily supplements of proteins and amino acids that will be immediately assim-ilated into the bloodstream and allow the body to know it's been satisfied but not stuffed.

Developing Health as a Habit

In 2007, schools will expand their concept of the words "physical education" to include up-to-date lessons in nutrition, the connections between health and diet, the relative ease of a habitually healthy relationship with well-chosen food compared to the constant battle of going on one diet after another, and a school-funded analysis of each student's basic physiological makeup so that students can learn early on how their nutritional needs may differ from their classmates' and what to do about it. Just as many children are currently teaching their clueless parents how to use computers, by 2010 many children will be teaching their parents better eating habits.

Physical education in schools will also become more personalized by 2010 to embrace the differences and individual interests of each child in the class. A full hour of movement will be offered by qualified teachers as awareness grows that asking some children to participate in a full hour of running, or a full hour of gymnastics or other highly strenuous exercise, isn't just setting them up to fail, it could actually be dangerous for them. Yoga, basic dance and certain martial arts will also be taught and valued for their potentially lifelong physical, emotional and disciplinary benefits, and children who once dreaded physical education class will finally start looking forward to it as an hour during the day that they can enjoy and where they can excel.

Intolerance for unhealthiness will spread to the workplace by 2012. Vending machines and regular food delivery services will offer exclusively healthy options or none at all—potato chips at the push of a button or delivery personnel bringing huge tins of pretzels and cookies every month will look in retrospect like the unfortunate trap it really is. And employers will catch on that their employees will be more productive if, during every weekday, there's a mandated thirty minutes set aside for some form of exercise. Again, as with students in physical education class, the point will be movement, not strenuous exercise, according to each employee's preference, interest and ability. Mind you, employers will be highly motivated to offer this mandated exercise break—if it's not set aside and adhered to, their companies will find themselves deprived of both insurance and workmen's comp availability. But who cares what motives trigger the progress, as long as it is achieved?

Medical Support

The diet drug industry is going to briefly get worse in the immediate future before it gets better, as certain unscrupulous thieves try to make the biggest, fastest money they possibly can before the majority of the public gets too well educated to fall for this nonsense anymore. In 2006 a medication will be developed and approved that will have a stimulating positive effect on the pancreas. It will help regulate blood sugar as well as, again, giving the body that feeling of being nutritionally satisfied, eliminating the compulsion to eat and keep eating without understanding why you're doing it. This medication, which is somehow injected or infused through the skin, is primarily a pure form of protein, with added vitamin and mineral supplements. Improvements on it in subsequent years will be tremendously instrumental in permanently stopping obesity and in regulating blood sugar levels so that hyper- and hypo- glycemia will cease to exist.

By 2012 every routine blood test from childhood on will include detailed profiles of any nutritional deficiencies our bodies are experiencing, and the highly advanced sup- plements that will be available by then to satisfy those deficiencies will be taken ser- iously and covered by insurance. Those same tests will include precise readings on our glands, organs, hormones and all body functions without our having to see special- ist after specialist to find out why, let's say, our bodies don't seem to be processing food as well as we know they should. I've experienced the same thing I'm sure many of you have, where I knew something was wrong and kept getting a long list of the word "normal" on blood test results until fi- nally the right specialist made the right re- quests of the right lab and, sure enough, it turned out one of those "normals" wasn't normal on closer inspection with more finely tuned technicians and equipment. So in 2012, many of those mysteries about what we're eating too much of or not enough of, or whether our thyroid is as active as it should be, or why our metabolism seems too slow for our activity level will be solved with a simple routine blood test that will be a habitual part of our lives from the time we're children.

Equally exciting will be the development in 2014 of a simple pill or capsule of some kind that will completely replace stomach-shrinking surgery, also known as gastric by-pass surgery. It will be safe and only necessary in cases of morbid obesity, which by then will be so rare as to be almost unheard of. Anorexia and bulimia will be eliminated in that same year, through the use of a medication that targets the pituitary gland.

And as we mentioned in Chapter 12, the positive effects of magnets on the body will be more widely understood and expanded on with every passing year, so that as soon as 2007, magnets will be used to stimulate such food-processing essentials of the body as the thyroid gland, the adrenal gland, the pancreas, the pituitary gland, the general digestive system and even the basic metabolism.

Now, I'm not sure how I feel about this next development. It's certainly harmless enough, and the principle behind it has been used before with what I guess could be called dubious success. There's going to be a bed pillow on the market in 2006 designed in such a way that you can program it to play any number of subliminal messages while you sleep, from lessons on health and nutrition to motivational tapes for diet and exercise.

It might be a great idea. It might be very helpful to a lot of people, in which case I say more power to it.

But I won't be buying one. It has nothing to do with skepticism or disinterest in learning about health and nutrition while I sleep.

It's just that the last thing I need in this world is one more voice in my head that isn't mine.

Exercise and Body Structure

There are those of you who hope I'm going to announce an upcoming pill that will make all forms of exercise completely unnecessary. Sorry. No such luck.

We do, though, have a never-ending array of innovations ahead in the world of exercise equipment. The first model of the breakthrough machine from which countless enhancements will follow makes its debut in about 2015. It's relatively compact considering how multifunctional it is, but I don't have a specific description beyond that. What I do have is a few details about the brilliant computer that constitutes the brain of this machine. To activate the computer and the machine, the user stands on a small floor-level platform that resembles a bathroom scale and tells the computer how much or little workout experience that person has had, how long it's been since the last workout, how often he or she would like to begin working out and what the goals are (weight loss, muscle tone, increase in stamina, general health improvement, and so on). The computer then designs an appropriate, well-rounded, personalized workout for that user, based not only on that information but also on a full-body analysis, essentially an "instant physical," that includes the user's strengths, weaknesses and special needs and protects him or her from strain or injury. The computer, not the user, manipulates the machine and the workout, a kind of ultimate personal trainer with medical expertise. These machines will be affordable and as common in homes as they are in gyms and health clubs, and because they're so highly personalized and effective, they'll actually be used, unlike the treadmills and other exercise machines that are gathering dust in countless homes today.

Eastern disciplines like yoga and the full range of martial arts will enjoy consistent popularity as well, decade after decade, as they have for centuries, and there will also be a form of passive exercise, starting in about 2008, in which machines send carefully controlled stimulation to various muscle groups, exercising them and increasing circulation. Unlike existing versions of these machines, the 2008 version will actually be effective.

In 2012 a body-shaping machine will be unveiled. It uses high-powered lights or laser beams that penetrate the body only as deep as the layer of fat beneath the skin. Over a course of ten or twelve sessions the beams break down or melt the layer of fat into a loose, gelatinous form that can be absorbed into the bloodstream and eliminated as waste. I'll still be around in 2012, so let me just add for the record that when this body shaper becomes available, you're more than welcome to get in line behind me, got it?

Maybe the most encouraging news of all about the future when it comes to our body structure is that by around 2030, our average height is going to have increased by several inches. The current average height of women in America is about five feet, four inches, while American men average approximately five feet, nine inches. In 2030, the average American woman will stand five-nine, and the average American man will be approximately six-one to six-three. If you're wondering why that's encouraging, the answer is that there's a known correlation between height and health. It goes something like "The more nutritious the food and the lower the pervasiveness of disease, the taller the population."

There's no doubt about it that we're not exactly excelling these days in the areas of diet, nutrition and fitness. Some percentage of it is our fault, for laziness, or lack of discipline, or our instant gratification mentality that demands a quick fix where none exists, or not demanding to be better informed, or simply letting ourselves pretend that we don't mind feeling less than the best we can. A greater percentage of it is the fault of too much confusing information, too much deceit on grocery store shelves to make money at the expense of our health, too little early education about nutrition and fitness, too many cookie-cutter blood tests, lab results and exercise regimens and too many "guaranteed" diets and pills that, when they fail, are so discouraging that people eventually give up and decide that fitness is something that's apparently meant for other people but sadly not for them.

No, there's no doubt about it, we can definitely do better. But remember, slowly but surely, as the years go by and we ease our way toward 2030, we're going to be getting taller and taller. Which means there's also no doubt about it that we *will* do better.

And unlike a lot of the other prophecies in this book, doing better with our diets, nutrition and fitness happens to be one prophecy we don't have to wait for. We can start right now. In fact, I know some of you will, and I want to hear about it.

Plastic Surgery

The key to the future of plastic surgery for both the face and the body is the laser, which by 2015 will be able to work beneath the skin to stimulate cells and natural collagen to allow literal reshaping and sculpting around the bone structure. Except in cases of extreme disfigurement, it will be a completely noninvasive procedure with a recovery time of a day or two at most.

Two or three preliminary consultations with a specialist will be required before any procedure takes place, partly because impulsive procedures are frowned on but mostly because it's imperative that the specialist and the patient are in complete agreement about the patient's goals. At each consultation, a hologram image of the patient's face and/or relevant body part(s) is projected for the specialist and the patient to study and make adjustments on together. Not until they both agree that the image is what the patient wants and what the specialist is legally and morally allowed to create will they schedule the procedure.

Today, for example, it's a popular fad

among young girls to be made to look as much like their favorite pop star idol as possible. And before we more mature women start throwing stones, we've got to admit we've seen our share of attempts at Elizabeth Taylor and/or Audrey Hepburn and/or Sophia Loren look-alikes walking down the street. The desire to look like a celebrity you admire is no big surprise. The big surprise is that it's legal today for plastic surgeons to participate in trying to make it happen, when one of the most rampant crimes on the planet is identity theft. In 2015, women and men will still be able to ask to be made to look like one of their favorite celebrities. But specialists will only legally be able to proceed if that celebrity is no longer living.

Specialists will also have the discretion to refuse a look-alike request they find morally disturbing, or that they believe could cause their patient physical or emotional harm. Someone wanting to be transformed into an Adolf Hitler duplicate, for example, or Ted Bundy, or Aileen Wuornos (America's most prolific female serial killer) will be promptly escorted from the office, or the specialist will be stripped of his or her credentials and prosecuted.

And speaking of those credentials, every specialist who performs plastic surgery will be required to have a medical degree, followed by two years of training with the equipment involved. Not only is the equipment unbelievably complicated and technical, but it's also hilariously expensive, which, please God, will keep it out of the hands of every quack who smells a quick, easy way to make a fortune.

So. Once those conditions have been satisfied and the specialist and patient are happy with the hologram image they've collaborated on, that image will be programmed into the computer of the machine that will perform the procedure. The computer will then make all the requisite calculations necessary, based on each patient's specific bone and cell structure, collagen and hormone levels, and so on, to accomplish the image.

When the computer signals that it's finished its work and fed the information to the microscopically precise machine, the patient, anesthetized with a mild tranquilizing skin patch, lies down on a glass table with a curved, hinged glass "roof" that closes over him or her, very much like a tanning bed or a small variation on the MRI machine. Laser sensors safely installed behind the glass in the "roof" and bed, preprogrammed by the computer to the specifications of the holo-gram image, will then go to work to dupli-cate that image. The specialist will be posi-tioned at a computer and screen nearby, tracking every move the machine makes, able to do fine-tuning on the procedure and to override the machine itself in the almost nonexistent event of any malfunction.

Again, the recovery time will be one to two days at most, and the results, some of which will be visible immediately, will con-tinue to manifest themselves gradually as the cells, collagen and hormone levels, and so on, make their adjustments, until the full effect is achieved, in approximately six weeks.

What I'd like to know is, where was this machine when I had my nose done? Not that I didn't, and don't still, love my plastic surgeon, but who's got time anymore to lie around for that long, looking like you've been dragged through a parking lot by your face?

In case you're wondering, this machine is much more sophisticated and intensive than the body-shaping machine we discussed in the exercise section. The difference is comparable to current liposuction, let's say, versus an exercise regimen on the most high-tech equipment available. They'll both accomplish the same result, but the two processes don't even slightly resemble each other.

A Word About Jewelry and Tattoos

Don't worry, a lot of this extreme body piercing will be out of style by about 2007, although tattooing is actually going to become even more popular and more artistic by around 2010.

We're also going to start wearing less and less jewelry by sometime around 2018, but what I find really interesting is that most of us will have at least one piercing on our bodies. The majority of us will go right on using those piercings for earrings. Some more adventurous (or masochistic) souls will continue to choose their noses, tongues or more discreet body parts. And these piercings will serve a dual purpose. Not only will they be decorative, but they'll also provide safe housing for microchips containing all of our personal information—name, address, Social Security number, driver's license number, blood type, Medic-Alert and insurance information, person to contact in case of emergency, and so on. This microchip can be detected and read by a small scanner that will be installed in every emergency vehicle, hospital, doctor's office and police car.

Yes, exactly like we routinely provide for our dogs and cats now, which I'm sure already occurred to a whole lot of you. So wouldn't you think . . . ?

I'm sure I don't even need to finish that question.

CHAPTER FOURTEEN

✳

Mental Health

The most exciting headline about the future status of mental health in our society is that it's going to finally be dealt with as a viable, legitimate *health* issue, as opposed to its current status as some vague, mysterious, uncomfortable "other" on our medical history forms that we'd rather not discuss. The day will come when we're as eager to acknowledge and be treated for a mental health problem as we are for a physical health problem, and as far as I'm concerned that day can't come a moment too soon. As it is now, it's a breeze to prove that we don't look at mental and physical health problems in remotely the same way: imag-

ine only confiding in your closest friends
that a family member has been diagnosed
with diabetes, let's say, instead of bipolarism, or hiding your allergy medication along
with your antidepressants in the back of
your sock drawer.

Do you realize how unapologetically attentive we are to every square inch of ourselves from the neck up except our brains,
without which those other square inches
wouldn't mean a thing? Eyes, ears, nose,
throat, complexion, teeth, wrinkles, hair—
one hint of trouble with any of those and
there's no amount of time or money we
won't spend to take care of it. A brain malfunction, in ourselves or a loved one? With
a few exceptions, we'll move heaven and
earth to ignore it until and unless addressing it becomes unavoidable.

One of those exceptions, thank God, is
Alzheimer's disease and the heartbreaking
mental short circuits it causes. Maybe it's
because those mental short circuits have a
medically identified and sanctioned disease
as their cause. Maybe it's because a lot of
brave souls have widely publicized their
painful challenges with loved ones who, because of Alzheimer's, are desperately dis-

oriented, have lost their memories and often no longer recognize their own spouses, children, siblings or grandchildren. I know the pain of being stared at like a stranger by someone who'd loved me all my life, and it's excruciating. I also know that, right or wrong, the fact that the person's loss of mental functions had a familiar, sympathetic physiological cause called Alzheimer's disease removed the stigma and made it easier for everyone to talk about.

Of course, almost all mental and psychological illnesses have physiological and/or neurological causes, which is a pretty widely known and understood certainty by now, so this centuries-old stigma makes no sense anymore anyway. In fact, it's embarrassing, foolish, unfair, unacceptable and antiquated, and the more we cling to the stigma the more we're shooting ourselves in the collective foot. The more active, vocal, well-informed interest we show in our mental health, the more responsive the medical, pharmaceutical, psychiatric, neurological and psychopharmaceutical professions will be. You don't need me to tell you that's true. All you have to do is stop and remember that none of us will put up with cold or flu symptoms for more than about five minutes without being ready to take medicine to get rid of them, and then check out the endless rows of cold and flu medicines available on store shelves. Let's face it, if we consumers create a profitable market for something, we can rest assured it's going to become more available than we ever dared hope, and then some.

Don't misunderstand for one second— I'm not talking about diagnosing our own mental illnesses, and I'm certainly not talking about self-prescribing medications supposedly geared toward improving our mental health and well-being. What I am talking about is exciting work being done in the mental health arena that I know about through friends and colleagues in that field, and even more advancements that I know we have to look forward to in the future. We can speed those advancements along considerably if we take the enthusiastic approach of "Of course I want to be as mentally healthy as possible. How do I go about it?" rather than the still-too-common "For one thing, there is nothing wrong with me mentally, thank you very much, and for another thing, how dare you imply that I'm crazy?"

Again I say—since most problems are very probably caused by something physiological and/or neurological that we may have been genetically predisposed to and that aren't remotely our fault to begin with, could we please drop the defensiveness and embarrassment and get on with the business of taking care of ourselves?

Diagnosing Mental Problems

I can't stress this enough: I have no psychological, psychiatric, neurological, medical or pharmaceutical qualifications, certificates or degrees. So I have no business making mental illness diagnoses or prescription recommendations of any kind. Unfortunately, neither do a lot of people who are diagnosing mental illnesses and prescribing medications to treat them. The difference is, they're doing it for a living, and their qualifications on paper might be perfectly legitimate. But I don't think there's a psychologist, psychiatrist, neurologist, physician or psychopharmacologist who

would disagree with me that there are prac-
titioners in each of those fields who are lazy,
uninformed, greedy, overworked, irrespon-
sible, in need of a career change or some
combination of the above. The result is either superficial or wrong diagnoses and
prescriptions that could be useless, harmful
or even fatal.

The truth is, not every child with behavior
problems has ADHD (we could probably all
say it in unison: Attention Deficit Hyperac-
tivity Disorder) and needs to take Ritalin. (I
haven't taken a poll on this, but I'm willing
to bet ADHD is one of the most overdiag-
nosed disorders and Ritalin is one of the
most overprescribed medications in this
country. Ritalin can work. It can also lead to
emotional disaster, addiction and death.)
Not every antidepressant is going to have a
positive effect on every person who's depressed, nor is every antianxiety medication
a good idea for everyone who suffers from
an anxiety disorder. There are several variations on bipolarism and schizophrenia and
several prescription medications available
for each of them, but the wrong medication
can exacerbate an already precarious problem. In other words, everywhere you turn,

there's no room for the careless or dispassionate in the mental health industry, where the stakes are already high enough to begin with.

On the flip side, there are just as many brilliant, dedicated professionals in that same industry, and it's our responsibility to find them, through referrals from other doctors we trust or friends who got results from whomever they're recommending. But the problem is, even the best and the brightest in the business may occasionally have a tough time diagnosing and prescribing, because mental and emotional disorders can be complex, unpredictable, disguised, deeply buried and/or a combination of disorders that each need treatment.

An enormous amount of biological, physiological and neurological research has been done and is being done to uncover definitive medical tests that will lead to more precise diagnoses of mental and emotional problems.

That research will pay off in countless ways. And it's imperative that we be receptive and willing to take full advantage of it.

In about 2009 there will be a significant breakthrough in connecting specific mental dysfunctions with specific physiological protein deficiencies and chemical imbalances that can be quickly and easily determined by blood tests and just as quickly and easily corrected with proper medication. I'm no scientist, and I can't begin to guess how many human proteins there are or how each of them functions in our bodies. But hypothetically, research will lead to the discovery that, let's say, deficiencies in the hemoglobin, elastase and cathepsin proteins, combined with elevated levels of amino acids, add up to obsessive-compulsive disorder, while too much haptoglobin and not enough natural insulin are a dead giveaway for clinical depression.

Not only will this take a lot of the guesswork out of diagnosing these problems, but it will also take a lot of the guesswork out of treating them. Once the elevated or deficient proteins and chemicals have been identified, they can be balanced and regulated with specific pills, injections or patches to control or even eliminate the mental disorder once and for all.

Antidepressants and antianxiety medications will also be more precisely manufactured and prescribed thanks to the ability to isolate protein and chemical imbalances and connect them to specific difficulties. Ask anyone who takes antidepressants if they were happy with the first one their doctor prescribed. I don't know one person who would answer yes to that question. In fact, it took one friend five different antidepressants to find one that worked for her, and the first four her doctor recommended were disasters in some form or other. One made her feel like she was living in a fog. Another kept her so sleepy she could barely get out of bed in the morning. The third actually increased her depression, and the fourth made her so apathetic that, looking back, she realizes she no longer even cared whether she was depressed or not. The fifth changed her life, thank God, and she's thriving on it. But what a dangerous, time-consuming, discouraging and exhausting crapshoot to go through to find the right medication, and the precision of the protein/chemical-balance blood test breakthrough will eventually eliminate that nonsense once and for all.

By far one of the most thrilling outcomes of this breakthrough will be the diagnosis and treatment of newborn infants through the same blood tests that are routinely taken now to indicate any medical and physiological problems. It's almost impossible to imagine what a difference it will make in the lives of those children, their families, and this world for that matter, when a whole range of psychological malfunctions is addressed within the first few days of a baby's birth, thanks to nothing more than protein and natural-body-chemical panels being added to the lab work on the infant's blood tests.

Again, we just have to be willing to take advantage of these opportunities when they come along. Sadly, or incredibly, some parents will refuse the protein and chemical aspects of the infancy blood test, out of fear or denial that there could be anything psychologically wrong with their child. That's one of the countless reasons we have to get rid of this inane stigma about mental disorders. Those same parents will leap at the opportunity to know about any medical problems their newborn baby might develop, so that something can be done immediately. But mental problems? When something can be done about those just as easily? The technology will be put into use in 2009, as I said, but it will be around 2012 before the percentage of parents giving permission for their infant's added protein and chemical blood panels rises above 90 percent.

Brain Disorders

Obviously, there are some mental illnesses whose primary source can be traced to that infinitely complex world called the brain. I feel safe in saying that humankind has been trying to unravel the mysteries of the brain since right around the time we realized we had one, and we've still only learned a fraction of all there is to know. So trying to diagnose and treat complicated dysfunctions with roots in an organ we don't understand much about to begin with is a huge challenge.

Schizophrenia is one of those dysfunctions. It's a severe, chronic brain disease that's probably caused by a series of chemical and neurological short circuits in the brain. Some studies have also led to the discovery of subtle abnormalities in the brain structure of many, but not all, schizophrenics. Still more studies are focusing on possible prenatal and genetic signals of a predisposition to schizophrenia. In other words, researchers are hard at work trying to figure out what on earth triggers it, but none of them disagree that the brain is where the core of the nightmare lies.

Contrary to popular belief, schizophrenia has nothing to do with having a split personality. It's an illness in which the person suffering from it loses the ability to tell the difference between reality and illusion. The person might see visions and hear voices that he or she will never believe are imaginary, and/or have irrational delusions of being very famous or that some random television or radio show is actually transmitting subliminal messages meant specifically for the schizophrenic, that he or she is the target of some vast government assassination plot or neighbors who are trying to brainwash the person for use in an intricate extraterrestrial conspiracy. Sadly, schizophrenics tend to divide the world around them into two groups of people: those who agree with them to placate them, and those who try to point out how ill they are and how urgently they need help—and that second group is likely to be dismissed as being part of "them," part of the "plot" or "conspiracy" or whatever delusion has become the schizophrenic's reality. Not for a moment do these people usually believe there's anything wrong with them, so convincing them to take medication tends to be a long shot at best, even though advancements are being made by leaps and bounds in psychopharmacological help for schizophrenics.

And then there's bipolar disorder, or manic depression, which is also a brain-related illness. It's not as severe as schizophrenia, but it can be just as destructive if it's not treated. A psychiatrist friend of mine describes it as the normal ups and downs all of us go through, except that both the ups and the downs are multiplied by about a hundred. The ups are almost overly euphoric, and the lows are such a rock-bottom sense of hopelessness that thoughts of suicide aren't all that uncommon. Those same ups can quickly turn to irritability, anger, aggression and inappropriate behavior. The downs can stop short of thoughts of suicide but still consume manic-depressives with chronic fatigue, a complete loss of interest in things they used to find exciting, overwhelming feelings of guilt and either a desire to sleep all the time or an inability to sleep at all. There are some excellent medications available for bipolar disorder. But again, the disorder has to be diagnosed correctly in the first place, which isn't always easy with this particular illness. And the manic-depressive has to believe that he or she is suffering from a treatable disease, which people with this illness are not always willing to do.

A personal note: I'll never forget the effect my first psychology class had on me, when I was a freshman in college. All I had to do was read a list of symptoms in that textbook and I'd become convinced that I had whatever mental illness those symptoms applied to. If you just read the above paragraph and felt a growing sense of panic that you might have bipolar disorder because you've experienced euphoria, anger, fatigue, guilt, disinterest, an inability to sleep, and so on in your life, take it from me, the simple fact that you're wondering is probably a good sign. And it's normal to experience each of those things from time to time. It's a matter of degree. Any mental health professional will back me up on that. But speaking of mental health professionals, if you find yourself sincerely concerned about yourself or a loved one, remember everything you've just read about how tough it is for experts to diagnose mental illnesses, and then imagine the odds against your being able to do a better job of it than they can. Run, don't walk, to a qualified professional and ask for help before you waste one moment trying to figure out for yourself if something's seriously wrong.

The Future of Brain Disorder Treatments

One of the most exciting developments in the treatment of brain-related mental illnesses will be put into the exclusive use of highly trained psychiatrists and neurologists in around 2013. Ironically, this development is going to be a dramatically improved variation on an old, outdated, barbaric approach, because it will make use of electrical and magnetic stimulation.

My guess is that you just flashed on images of horror stories about shock treatments, bad movies with electrodes attached to screws in someone's skull and zombie-like people scuffing vacantly through snake-pit asylum hallways.

At any rate, comparing what's coming to what really was often cruel and inhumane is like comparing modern surgery to the days when doctors had their patients drink a nice big shot of whiskey and bite on a bullet in preparation for a procedure. (Or so I've heard. I'm not *that* old.) This new device is going to operate much like an MRI machine, in that it will glide slowly, smoothly and almost silently back and forth across the surface of the skull, from the top of the forehead to the nape of the neck. As it moves across the skull, it receives and responds to any abnormalities in the brain, the cerebrospinal fluid that surrounds the brain, blood circulation within the brain, and neurological and chemical activity in each hemisphere of the brain and between the two hemispheres, the individual lobes, and so on.

Wherever the device detects an abnormality, it signals the neurologist or psychiatrist who's administering the treatment and viewing the details of the scan on a computer screen with its own set of diagnostic readouts. At the same time, the device, through its own diagnostic settings, emits a series of electromagnetic impulses, of pinpoint precision and highly sensitive varying strength, at every malfunction it detects that will positively respond to stimulation—where circulation is slow, where the neurotransmitters are "misfiring" or dormant, where there's a conspicuous chemical imbalance—anywhere the device, with the specialist there to offer an immediate "second opinion," senses that electromagnetic stimulation will be beneficial.

Monthly treatments with this device, combined with medications specific to each patient based on blood tests revealing protein and chemical imbalances, will be as dramatic a contribution to the world of mental health as, let's say, DNA has been to the world of law enforcement. Bipolar disorder will be easily controlled into virtual nonexistence, and even depression, anxiety and other dysfunctions that don't seem to be as brain-originated will benefit by milder versions of stimulation from this same device.

As for schizophrenics, this brilliant device and the most custom-compounded medication the world has to offer still can't do a thing until and unless these poor people understand that they're ill, which isn't going to get any more likely in the future than it is now. But there's hope for them as well, and it will come as a result of some exciting brain research that's currently under way. Scientists are finding reason to believe that there may be a connection among bipolar disorder, schizophrenia and seizures. If that's true, and a common core of all three can be found, it could—and will—lead to a common way to control all three.

It will be in 2014 at the latest that a microchip will be invented and implanted in the brain of schizophrenics and those who have severe seizure and bipolar disorders. This microchip will be able to sense when any kind of malfunction, misfire, shutdown or break is about to occur in the brain and essentially "take over" and keep all systems up and operating until the brain is ready to kick into gear again. It will perform the same function for the brain that the pacemaker performs for the heart, and it will save more anguish and more lives than we can begin to calculate.

Schizophrenics with confirmed diagnoses from two separate psychiatrists and/or neurologists will most often receive the implant surgery by court order, either by their next of kin having them declared mentally incompetent or by the diagnosing professionals testifying that they are an immediate threat to their own lives or the lives of others. So denying their illness won't prevent schizophrenics any longer from finally getting the long-term, nearly miraculous help they need. I say "nearly" because this microchip won't clinically cure schizophrenia. Nothing will. But it will make it such a manageable illness that those who suffer from it will be healthy and functional enough to be willing to take any supplemental medication their doctors suggest.

The Ripple Effect of Future Treatments

Millions upon millions of people around the world, in every imaginable walk of life and financial circumstance, suffer from some form and degree of mental illness. The impact of diagnosis and precise treatment through protein and chemical blood tests, especially at birth, and of this future electromagnetic device and microchip, will be felt far beyond those millions and deep into every corner of society as the applications and repercussions of those treatments continue to spread.

* New York, Cleveland, Germany and Sweden will be on the cutting edge of these breakthroughs and, as a result, will become great centers for those in search of help for the most serious or complicated mental disorders.
* It will evolve that the specialties of psychiatry and neurology will form a close partnership and become the traditional diagnosis/treatment team in the mental health world. Thorough testing by both, separately and as a team, will be required by insurance companies for coverage of treatments, and it will be an industry mandate that electromagnetic treatments and microchip implants must have the endorsement of both professionals for each patient in question before those procedures are used.
* Pharmaceutical companies will enjoy a whole new flush of success in their

production of highly specific antidepressant and antianxiety medications
and their race to improve on electromagnetic treatment devices and microchips.

* Anorexia will be found to respond
very quickly and positively to a variation on the treatment used for schizophrenics.

* The criminal justice and prison systems will be dramatically transformed
by the ability to determine through
blood tests whether or not the potential for treatable and/or legitimate
mental illness exists. Faking insanity
will be eliminated as a defense option,
and transforming treatment into such
a precise and efficient process will
make it more available to prisoners
who can benefit from it.

* "Turfing" and other hushed practices
that have created mistrust in the mental health industry will become a thing
of the past. ("Turfing" is the industry
term for passing difficult and severely
troubled patients from one professional or institution to another or
"anywhere but here" when that pro-

fessional or institution gets too frustrated to keep trying. It's not something the industry takes pride in or even admits to easily, but they'd have trouble denying it under oath.) Again, diagnoses and treatments that work in the widest possible variety of illnesses will eliminate the pervasive sense of discouragement and futility that can occasionally overwhelm even the most brilliant, compassionate and gifted mental health professional. The greater the success rate, the less the motivation for handing off extreme cases to anyone/anywhere else.

* Blood tests for protein and chemical imbalances and deficiencies in newborns will be so effective in producing mentally healthier children, adolescents and adults that by 2015 those same tests will be performed in the womb through amniocentesis so that the fetus can actually begin receiving mild treatments through nutritional supplements in utero.

* By 2017 the stigma of mental illness will be gone, and the worldwide embracing of the protein/chemical blood

tests will be so appropriately entrenched that monthly home blood testing kits for protein/chemical levels will be as common as home testing kits for insulin levels are today.

The Future Role of Psychologists

Without the added education and medical degrees required for psychiatry, psychologists, unable to participate in the diagnosis/treatment advancements of blood testing, electromagnetic therapy and microchip implants, will obviously continue working with the wealth of people whose problems are circumstantial or self-imposed but not physiologically caused.

But with groundbreaking industry breakthroughs going on all around them, and a much more open-minded, well-informed public demanding more efficient results, psychologists will have to come up with some effective breakthroughs of their own or get left in the dust. I can't tell you how often I've heard clients say something like "I have the most wonderful therapist. I've been seeing him/her twice a week for over fifteen years now." Trust me, by as soon as 2010, only a handful of people in search of help will find anything "wonderful" about a psychologist who eats up that much time and I shudder to think how much money.

I swear to you, the breakthrough that more and more psychologists, even the most conservative and traditional ones, will begin putting into use is hypnotherapy for the specific purpose of past-life regressions. I know, I know. Some of you don't believe in past lives, and even more of you who happen to be seeing therapists are imagining your sessions being doubled in frequency if you strolled in and announced that a psychic suggested you try hypnotic past-life regressions.

I repeat, I'm not a psychologist, psychiatrist or trained medical practitioner of any kind. I am, however, a certified master hypnotist. I've done literally thousands and thousands of hypnotic past-life regressions over these last many decades, and I've seen how quickly and permanently they've helped to rid clients of countless fears, guilt, chronic aches and pains, recurring nightmares, unhealthy attractions and aversions, and on and on that would never have been dealt with by traditional means because they weren't rooted in this particular lifetime.

Not only is hypnotic past-life regression efficient and effective, but another of its many bonuses is that you don't even have to believe in it for it to work. And if your therapist is open to the possibility of exploring it, the responsibility of the study, work and training will fall to the therapist, not to you. This specific type of regression requires more than just a certificate or diploma in hypnotherapy. I've personally trained enough hypnotic past-life regressionists to assure you that it's a specific skill, requiring, just for starters, an instinct for the right questions to ask and when to ask them, the ability to encourage but never "lead" the client's journey, knowledge of the basics the client is experiencing, and the compassion to know when to let the client go through something that's upsetting and when to stop and help the client move on to something else. In my book *Past Lives, Future Healing,* for example, which deals exclusively with this subject, I commented on the fact that I've never had a client go through too much difficulty over his or her death in any past life, but I've stopped letting clients go anywhere near the one experience that's consistently much too horrifying for them to deal with under hypnosis, which is their birth into this life. If you want to see even the strongest, toughest, most cynical skeptic in the world reduced to a sweaty, panic-stricken pile of emotional rubble, have that person relive being born.

It's not just the novelty of experiencing moments from past lives, past deaths or our real lives on the Other Side that's so valuable to clients, and that will be so valuable to psychologists as more and more of them begin using hypnotic past-life regression as a therapy tool. It's also a fascinating biological/physiological/spiritual reality called cell memory.

To understand cell memory you have to understand a couple of basic facts. One is that every one of the billions of cells in our body is a living, breathing, viable organism that reacts instantly and literally to the information it receives from the subconscious mind. We know it's not the conscious mind that controls what our cells do—when, for example, was the last time you consciously gave orders to the cells in your pancreas about how to proceed with their responsibilities at any given moment? Thank *God* it's not our forgetful, procrastinating, easily preoccupied conscious minds but our subconscious ones that control the cell functions of our bodies, or the average human life span would be about three minutes.

At any rate, the other basic fact about cell memory is that our spirit minds, that part of us God created that is eternal, are kept safe and completely intact in our subconscious minds while we're occupying bodies here on earth. Now, unless you believe that you came into this lifetime and into this body from absolute nowhere and nothingness (which you can't believe if you believe in eternity—it's either one or the other), you know that your spirit mind remembers perfectly everywhere it's been before it got here and will remember this life perfectly when it leaves and goes Home again.

One of the common areas of confusion about past lives I should clear up before we go any further, I think, is that they're really not separate lives as their name implies. They're all simply phases of the one same eternal life that each of us is given. Your toddler years, kindergarten, adolescence and first job, let's say, are all vastly different experiences in this current lifetime you're living, but not "separate" at all. In exactly the same way, every other lifetime you've lived, here on earth, on the Other Side, and again this time around, is simply a different experience in one eternal continuum. Through every past, present and future lifetime in that continuum, we're never anyone but *us*.

The most natural state of existence for our spirit minds is in the spirit world of the Other Side. On those occasions when we choose to make brief trips to earth, we're going to find ourselves in the relatively unnatural but oddly familiar temporary confines of a human body again for the duration. The minute that oddly familiar reentry happens, while our body is still in the womb, our spirit mind is flooded with memories of every other time we've been in those same dense, earthbound confines. The spirit mind, intertwined with the subconscious as it is, immediately starts sending signals to the cells based on all those memories, and the cells, which don't know the past from the present from the future and only process the information they're given without judging, respond accordingly, and the result is cell memory.

If you've ever revisited the house where you spent your childhood, or the halls of your grade school, or the first church or synagogue you attended, and felt a surge of overwhelming emotions and long-forgotten memories that instantly reconnect you with a whole other part of yourself you thought you'd lost track of, you've experienced a fraction of what the spirit mind feels when it finds itself inhabiting a human body again. It doesn't matter that the spirit mind chose to inhabit that body and made exhaustive plans for it ahead of time, any more than it matters how much you prepared yourself for a reunion with one of your old childhood "haunts." The impact can be huge and pervasive, good or bad, and its suddenness is just an inevitable part of the overall long-lasting effect.

Let's say that in your lifetime on earth preceding this one, your death was caused by an accidental drowning when you were forty years old. Your spirit mind now finds itself in a very mortal human body again after maybe a century or two of bliss on the Other Side, and one of its many reactions as it realizes where it is and adjusts is bound to be some version of "And last time I was in this situation I drowned when I was forty." The subconscious mind gets the message, which sends it on to each and every cell, that either a lifelong fear of water or an escalating fear of water as you get closer to forty might be very appropriate, and that developing serious mortality issues in your thirties might make all the sense in the world. Your spirit mind, in other words, begins inadvertently anticipating and bracing for something it's already experienced, not necessarily relevant to this lifetime at all.

I can tell you from personal experience with client after client after client, times thousands, that uncovering that past-life drowning at forty, letting the client reexperience it just long enough to see that it's something that's behind, not ahead, and that the client clearly went right on from there to the Other Side and even back here to earth again, releases the fear of water, the phobia about turning forty and most often the fear of death as well.

Again, with so many of our current emotional and even chronic physical problems directly traceable to cell memories, and quickly and effectively solved by uncovering, examining and releasing those cell memories through hypnosis, how effective are psychologists likely to be if they continue to take the approach that we didn't exist before our birth into this life?

I didn't invent cell memory. I don't have a patent on it. I have nothing to gain by being such a passionate advocate of its being accepted and given a sincere, healthy try by psychologists who agree with me that the greatest service you can offer your clients is the maximum amount of life-altering help in the briefest possible amount of time.

Hypnotic past-life regression will become available through a select number of trained psychologists on the east and west coasts and throughout Europe by 2009, and by virtue of its remarkable success it will become a widely practiced, sought-after skill by 2011.

I'll still be doing readings and my own past-life regressions then, so it's going to cost me clients, but you won't hear one word of complaint. In fact, all you'll hear, from me, and from the thousands of clients who've released their own past-life fears, traumas and heartaches right before my eyes and never been bothered by them again is—*it's about time!*

CHAPTER FIFTEEN

✳

Relationships

I want you to know that even with all the current unrest in the world, even with our country at war, our economy weak and un-employment rampant, the one question I'm still asked by clients more often than any other is "When am I going to meet Mr./Ms. Right?"

On one hand, I completely understand. The desire to find a special person to share your life with has been alive on this planet for as long as we humans have. In fact, believe me when I tell you, been there, done that.

On the other hand, I find myself looking around and marveling at how generally inept we humans are at navigating our way through relationships in such a way that they won't just last, they'll last because they *should* last. They'll last because, thanks to mutual trust and respect and support and appreciation and sense of responsibility, the two people involved in the relationship actually enhance each other's life instead of just complicating it or distracting each other.

We've had thousands and thousands of years to make the same relationship mistakes over and over and over and over again and learn from them.

You'd think we'd get better at it.

Maybe it's something we have to look forward to.

Don't be silly. We're going to be as awkward as ever.

We're just going to do some restructuring and see if that helps.

The Future of Dating

We'll never stop running into people we're attracted to, and maybe going out with them a few times. That's not what I mean when I talk about dating. Dating in this discussion means two people seeing each other with the expressed or implied intention of developing a significant relationship that will last for a long period of time.

By 2012 we will have exhausted our patience with ourselves, our choices of the partners we've invested in for potential relationships and our random methods of seeking out those choices. We've long since stopped complaining about how we never have the time or the opportunity to meet anyone, because now, of course, there's cyberspace, where we can quite literally meet more people than we know what to do with. And many of them seem every bit as eager to find and settle down with a significant other as we are. Too eager, in some cases. Almost suspiciously eager, if we didn't know better. Which, come to think of it, we don't. But we personally know two couples who met on the Internet and couldn't be happier, so there's proof that it can happen—as long as we ignore the fifteen or twenty people we also know who met someone on the Internet and ended up getting ripped off for hundreds or thousands of dollars, having their identity stolen,

being harassed to the point of near-stalk-
ing, discovering that this single person of
their dreams was really married with six
children and no job, discovering that this
single person of their dreams was really a
group of fourteen-year-olds with too much
time on their hands, or even relocating to
build a new life with this fabulous person
who was so kind and attentive and sexy in
cyberspace, only to discover that this fabulous person failed to mention in all those
e-mails that he or she lives like a pig, goes
days without taking a shower and occasionally likes to throw things and hit when
he or she gets angry.

Oddly, or maybe predictably, it's the
ridiculous hyper-availability of relationship
potential that will lead to the almost exclusive practice of dating through reputably
established dating services by 2012. These
will bear only a passing resemblance to the
dating services of today, because by 2012
we're all going to be more cautious than
ever, and rightly so. (Actually, let me clarify
that—people who take themselves and
their lives seriously are going to be more
cautious than ever. Those who don't aren't
likely to be reading this chapter anyway.) It

will take more than a business license, a binder full of photos and files of your clients' occupations and favorite hobbies to make a legitimate dating service a success in 2012. But if you're considering starting one around then and think you can do it right, by all means go for it, because you'll be in one of the most sought-after businesses in the country.

Dating service memberships in 2012 will not be inexpensive. A tiny fraction of the reason for that will be to try to keep out those who are just signing up on a whim because they're bored or in need of attention. But a much larger percentage of the cost will be due to the change in attitude at these services. Forget the prevailing attitude that the more clients you sign up the more successful matches you're likely to make, and/or that once clients get together, it's up to them to decide how much or how little or how quickly or how slowly they want to open up about themselves. In 2012, if a prospective client tries taking an "it's none of your business" attitude, the answer will be "oh, yes, it is, take it or leave it," no matter how much money the prospective client has, or how attractive or charming or what "great dating material" they seem to be.

At every legitimate dating service in 2012, the "service" you'll be paying for will include a guarantee that all the clients you're introduced to have been fingerprinted and had their prints run through a law enforcement database, to check for little details like outstanding warrants, criminal history and if they are who they say they are. They'll have been subjected to a thorough background check, to reveal marriages and divorces, child support judgments, bankruptcies, résumé verification, tax liens, repossessions and any other financial information that's a matter of public record—in other words, everything you should take the time to find out before you get involved with someone now, but probably don't bother. And yes, they'll also have to take and pass a drug test. So if you find someone in the files whose profile appeals to you, you can at least proceed with a reasonable assumption that the person is worth five minutes of your time, and the other person can proceed with the same reasonable assumption about you.

That's what lies ahead in the world of dating services. What do you think?

Have a huge pile of cash, but you'd never make it past the background check? Don't waste your time or theirs.

Could easily meet all the criteria, but you resent the invasion of your privacy? No problem. That's certainly your prerogative. Bye-bye.

Trust me, by 2012, the vast majority of singles in this country will have had quite enough of being fooled, and of making fools of themselves. In addition, though, in around 2009 there will be a well-publicized lawsuit against a dating service for matching up an attractive, seemingly successful man with a woman he ends up killing. It turns out the man was on parole from a second-degree murder and drug conviction. The dating service will be held partially responsible, through a version of the same theory that holds bars responsible for continuing to serve drinks to a customer who's clearly drunk.

From that court ruling on, as dating services become more closely scrutinized, they'll have no choice but to become more discerning, at the same time their potiential

clientele is experiencing the exact same necessity.

And by 2015, dating through cyberspace
will seem as reckless and foolish in retrospect as hitchhiking, which we used to not
think twice about a few decades ago,
seems to us now. Another excellent example of "just because we can doesn't mean
we *should*."

Nor will dating through cyberspace, or
anywhere else for that matter, seem quite
as urgent at that point anyway, since the
words "object: matrimony" will have started
to fade from everyone's consciousness.

Marriage

By 2020 we're going to see an end to the
institution of marriage as we know it.

I'm sure there were a few gasps when
you read that, and I admit I felt a bit of a
twinge when I wrote it. Then I started thinking long and hard about it and realized that
the twinge came from habit and sentiment
and my eternal romanticism, but in truth I
couldn't honestly say I was surprised or
even terribly sad that we as a society might

be coming up with an alternative to the current tradition of marriage.

The most recent statistic I read was that forty-nine out of every one hundred marriages end in divorce. If I were to go just by the clients I talk to in the course of a week, I would guess the percentage is higher than that. And let's face it, I've done my part to hold up my end of the statistics, with three divorces, or four if you count an annulment when I was in my teens, and we can put my cowriter and friend Lindsay down for one marriage, one divorce, and then there's my staff, and my family—who I'm not about to drag into this conversation, so never mind.

But it's not just statistics that are going to ultimately lead to the demise of marriage. It's also that, as anyone will tell you who's been through it, ending even a marriage you want out of can be one of the most emotionally and financially debilitating experiences you could ever be put through, to the point where you run screaming from the mere mention of the word "marriage" for the rest of your life no matter who's offering. (Take it from me.) It's also that staying married to spare yourself the trouble or expense or embarrassment of divorce, as many people do, let's face it, is even more emotionally debilitating than divorce itself, because in the end, it's a day in, day out lie, and that's no way to live. It's also that many people, and you can't disagree with me on this one, are so eager to get married because it's their idea of what they're supposed to do that they put more thought into which car to buy than they put into whom they should marry. And it's also that many people want to legitimize the children they're eager to have, only to either make those children miserable by splitting up after having them or make them miserable by staying together and hating each other.

I do know a few healthy, happy marriages. A very few. I marvel at them, and I applaud them. And I can say without a moment of hesitation that those couples would be together, equally healthy and happy, whether or not they'd ever formalized their relationship in the eyes of God and man.

In 2020 people will certainly be welcome to be united in civil ceremonies if they care to, don't get me wrong. But by then, children living with single parents will be so much more common than children living with both parents, and the stigma of children being "illegitimate" will be so archaic that couples forming a civil union will seem downright silly unless there are practical financial benefits in it for both people.

Now, please, please, *please* don't start mourning the loss of "family values" when the institution of marriage fades away in 2020. "Family values" can and will still be alive and well; they'll simply be redefined. The whole point of family values to begin with was the healthiest environment in which the children of two responsible parents could possibly be raised, right? That's certainly the way I understood it. I mean, it couldn't have been "the two biological parents and their children living under the same roof, no matter what, as long as they all go to church together on a regular basis." We've all seen that act disguise any number of horrors. And we also know far too many really wonderful people who had that exact intention, but circumstances took it away. They can't be judged for circumstances that aren't their fault to begin with, after all. So family values has to be about children being raised by responsible parents in the healthiest possible environment, doesn't it?

And they will be. Probably a healthier one, because eliminating marriage will eliminate the highly likely divorce, which will eliminate the equally likely custody battle. I've never seen a single child go through a custody battle without a whole lot of disruption, confusion and just plain hurt, and forgive the understatement, but *it's not fair.* With the divorce rate as it is now, how can we pretend that a custody battle isn't a likely extension of the current family values image?

(Which reminds me, did you know that the area of the country with the highest divorce rate happens to be the Bible belt? I'm not saying that proves anything, I was just surprised to learn that and thought you might be too.)

Unmarried couples who choose to have children together starting in the post-marriage 2020s, and who choose to do it responsibly, will visit a highly referred doctor for thorough blood and DNA tests, which by then will be able to foreshadow any possible genetic problems that can be medically corrected ahead of time with prenatal treatments. The couple will each provide thorough family physical and mental health histories that can also be factored into these tests. The babies resulting from these added precautions will be conspicuously healthier than babies born without those same preconception blood/DNA tests and family prenatal corrections. So even if I'm wrong (I'm not) and marriage retains its current popularity after 2020 (it won't), it will become standard practice for couples to go through preconception testing if they're even considering having children together.

I think it's going to be very difficult for lawmakers to outlaw gay marriage in the United States because I can't imagine how they're going to word a law that makes it legal to discriminate in a land in which, according to the Constitution, we're all equal. I'm sorry, but legally, this reminds me way too much of women being turned away from voting booths and African Americans not being able to use white people's water fountains.

Civil unions make more sense for all of us in this country, and they will be legalized for gay couples.

Be tolerant when that happens. And if you can't be tolerant, at least be smart. You could be part of some group that's arbitrarily singled out to be discriminated against someday, and you'll be hoping for that same tolerance if and when that happens.

The Return of Communal Living

Now that I've thoroughly irritated a lot of you, I might as well go ahead and irritate even more of you—although I'm not thrilled about this next part myself, so don't kill the messenger.

Following the demise of the institution of marriage and the subsequent realization that civil unions aren't serving that much of a purpose either, for either of the adults, it becomes acceptable by around 2050 for everyone to have several partners. Notice I said *everyone.* Yes, it's both men and women this time for whom multiple partners will eventually be acceptable, and it may or may not surprise you that men will have a harder time adjusting to this arrangement than women will. Technically, this won't amount to polygamy, because none of these partnerships will be formalized by marriage. What they will do is lead to a kind of natural evolution into a return to communal living. One man's four women, let's say, and those women's three men each, and those men's three or four women each begin moving closer to one another—you get the idea.

Children result from these partnerships, needless to say. But it's refreshing to note that, maybe because people have almost unlimited freedom, there's a remarkable amount of responsibility about birth control, and the children, almost without exception, are planned by two parents who are seriously interested in having them and raising them well. "It takes a village to raise a child" swings into action in the commune from the moment a baby arrives, and there's certainly no lack of love, attention and excellent schooling for the children in these groups, nor is there such a thing as deadbeat dads or moms—if failing to support their child even entered their mind they would be shamed out of town so fast they wouldn't know what hit them.

These tight-knit communities seem to work fairly well, for about one generation. Their like-mindedness in spiritual and survival matters creates an atmosphere in which they all seem to pull together and take care of one another, in a kind of one-for-all-and-all-for-one unity that has a lot to be said for it.

What's interesting, though, is that as the children begin reaching their late teens and early twenties, their ultra-involved and protective parents find themselves trying to handpick mates for them and being very emotionally resistant to the idea of their children entering into the same multiple partnerships the parents have set as a relationship example.

The "arranged couples" idea doesn't get any further than it ever has for any length of time in the United States. But what do you know, by 2075, multiple partnerships evolve back into a preference for monogamy again, because, in the end, no matter how many different ways we find to choreograph our lives, human nature never really changes all that much.

CHAPTER SIXTEEN

✳

Spirituality: The Benediction

The dictionary defines a benediction as "the invocation of a divine blessing." I can't think of a more perfect way to end this book.

From 2060 to 2100 I see a gorgeous period of peace, tolerance, understanding and profound global unity and compassion. It's as if all the countries around the world finally "get it" and feel the moral need to make up for the centuries of cruel, greedy, arrogant damage they've inflicted on one another at the expense of the only planet we humans have been given to care for and live these lives on.

From 2100 on I see nothing.

Does that mean we only have one hundred more years of life on this earth?

God only knows.

And I mean that as literally as you can possibly take it. God only knows. He's the only all-knowing One in this infinite, eternal universe.

All the rest of us can do is listen, pay attention, find the Light in ourselves and those around us and then, *for God's sake,* get out there together and shine that Light so brightly, He'll see that we finally understand what so many people have been trying to tell us for thousands and thousands of years:

We are all relations . . . The Sacred Mother (Earth) is screaming for life . . . Go to where the eagles fly, to where the wolf roams, to where the bear lives. Here you will find life because they will always go to where the water is pure and the air can be breathed. Live where the trees, the lungs of this earth, purify the air. There is a time coming, beyond the weather. The veil between the physical and the spiritual world is thinning.

—the Lakota Indians

It is time for the Great Purification. We are at a point of no return. The two-legged are about to bring destruction to life on Earth. It's happened before, and it's about to happen again. The Sacred Hoop shows how all things go in a circle. The old becomes new; the new becomes old. Everything repeats . . . Culture is having roots in the Earth. People without culture don't exist very long because Nature is God. Without a connection to Nature, the people drift, grow negative, destroy themselves. In the beginning we had one mind, and it was positive, a thing of beauty, seeing beauty everywhere.

—Brave Buffalo, the Sioux Nation

We've got to learn to love one another.
You see, that's really what's going to
   happen to the earth.
We're going to have tidal waves.
We're going to have earthquakes.
That's coming because we don't
   consider this land as our Mother.
We've taken away the balance, and
   we're not putting back.

               —the Aborigines

Follow your own footsteps.
Learn from the rivers,
the trees and the rocks.
Honor the Christ,
the Buddha,
your brothers and sisters.
Honor your Earth Mother and the Great
Spirit.
Honor yourself and all of creation.
Look with the eyes of your soul and
engage the essential.

—the Inca Q'ero shamans

Mankind can be saved by returning to its spiritual values.

—Sir Arthur Conan Doyle

If you go on with this nuclear arms race, all you are going to do is make the rubble bounce.

—Winston Churchill

Know self
by activities of self
in the daily walks of life,
by comparing
each thought
and activity by your standard

The Christ.
Be what thou
seemeth, live thy creed.
Hold up to the earth the torch
divine.
Be what thou
prayest to be made.
Let the Great Master's step be thine.
                                    —Edgar Cayce
                                (Reading 262:10)

That last quote of Edgar Cayce's wasn't mentioned earlier in this book because technically it's not a prophecy. But it's true, it's beautiful and it contains the answer to a question I get asked by clients every day: "People keep saying 'get in touch with your spirituality,' and I'd love nothing more than to get in touch with my spirituality, but the truth is, I don't even understand what they're talking about. What does 'getting in touch with my spirituality' really mean, and where do I start?"

Now, that's a great question. And a fair one. Haven't we all pretty much had it with rhetoric and lip service and dogma and "spin," with no meaningful, reliable actions to back them up? Or those impassioned answers that are "guaranteed" to bring you closer to yourself and to God, but all you feel closer to after you've tried them is your ability to fail at things that seem to come so easily to other people?

The great news is, there are lots of ways to find that return to spirituality that all those prophets have been urging us toward for so long. There is no such thing as the "right" way beyond discovering what works for you, what resonates so deeply inside you that you know it's reached your soul, what makes you *feel* instead of just "act," what, like the difference between fast food and a great meal, leaves you "satisfied" instead of just "full." What makes a difference in you that will last more than a couple of weeks or a month or until, as my friend Bernie puts it, the next "shiny object" comes along.

Many, as we know, find the path to their spirituality through regular attendance and involvement in their religion. That's been known to work for me, and there's not a day when I don't feel "involved" in Gnostic Christianity somehow. But I'll be honest, there are times, especially after a long road trip, when attending church feels like just one more place I have to be, and I sit through the service like a lump, wondering if I'm going to have time to squeeze in a nap before my sons and my grandchildren come over. Hardly what either God or I has in mind for a meaningful connection.

Many are wonderfully disciplined about daily meditation, and I couldn't be more in favor of that. I usually manage about five minutes of it, while I'm in my bedroom getting dressed in the morning. There's no mat. There are no candles. There's no incense, and there's certainly no tranquil sense of serenity. (In fact, there are usually so many dogs leaping around on me during it that I head for work looking like Bigfoot.) And I wouldn't necessarily describe those minutes as meditation, they're more like a quick regrouping between me and God, just to say hello, ask for His guidance and protection and promise to try not to disappoint Him.

There are extraordinary retreats, study groups both in person and online, counselors in every religion who, if you get to the right person, love nothing more than to help members and nonmembers alike find the path to God that makes sense to them.

Crystals? I love them. A friend of mine loved them too, and was so convinced that they enhanced her spiritual power that she wore a zillion of them around her neck at all times and ended up at the chiropractor.

And as for hugging trees—I'll tell you the truth, I've never hugged a tree in my life, I'm not especially planning on it, and I'm guessing trees appreciate it a lot more that I've also never destroyed one.

What I can honestly say works for me to keep my spirituality alive and well, and to keep myself satisfied instead of just full, and to keep my soul truly exhilarated, is put beautifully in that Edgar Cayce quote:

Be what thou prayest to be made.

If you pray that people become more compassionate, *become more compassionate.*

If you pray that people become more tolerant, *become more tolerant.*

If you pray that people become more honest, *become more honest.*

If you pray that people become more generous, *become more generous.*

If you pray that people start giving again,

to animals, to children, to the homeless, to the rain forests, to those with currently incurable diseases, to charities whose work you believe in, *start giving again.*

If you pray that this world becomes healthier, *become healthier.*

If you pray that this world becomes more peaceful, *become more peaceful.*

If you pray that this world and all of us who share it do far, far better than we have been, to repay our debt of gratitude to our loving God who knows the Way and is the Way, *do far, far better, to repay your debt of gratitude to God.*

Be what thou prayest to be made.

Finally, my own benediction, from my heart and spirit to yours, as the genetic brothers and sisters we are, sharing the same Creator:

Dear Mother and Father God, today please help us really look at the people and this earth around us, not to rush carelessly past them but to really see that they are, each and all, Your gifts to us, to cherish, to reach out our hand to and to protect from our own misguided sense of entitlement. Never again let us say that we have something more important to do than to take care of one another and of this beautiful, tattered planet. Help us remember that saying that means saying we have something more important to do than to take care of You, and in the depth of our spirits we know that's not true.

May the White Light of the Holy Spirit surround and bless us, and the sacred life of our dear earth, with Thy divine wisdom, compassion and peace. Amen.

A professional psychic for nearly fifty years, **Sylvia Browne** has written many tremendously successful books, including *The Other Side and Back* and most recently *Visits from the Afterlife.* She appears regularly on *Montel,* and her frequent lectures attract thousands of attendees. She lives in California.